KNIT
NORO

KNIT NORO

30 DESIGNS IN LIVING COLOR

sixth&spring books

sixth&spring ▪▪ books

161 Avenue of the Americas
New York, New York 10013
sixthandspringbooks.com

Managing Editor	**WENDY WILLIAMS**
Senior Editor	**MICHELLE BREDESON**
Yarn Editor	**RENEE LORION**
Instructions Editors	**JONI CONIGLIO**
	EVE NG
	MARY LOU EASTMAN
Instructions Proofreaders	**STEPHANIE MRSE**
	LORI STEINBERG
	LORETTA DACHMAN
	JONI CONIGLIO
	MARY LOU EASTMAN
	BONNIE ARNOLD
	TANA PAGELER
Technical Illustrations	**CHARLOTTE PARRY**
Photography	**ROSE CALLAHAN**
Stylist	**SARAH LIEBOWITZ**
Hair and Makeup	**LENA FOR MAKE UP FOREVER**
Vice President, Publisher	**TRISHA MALCOLM**
Creative Director	**JOE VIOR**
Production Manager	**DAVID JOINNIDES**
President	**ART JOINNIDES**

Knit Noro
30 Designs in Living Color
Sixth&Spring Books

**Library of Congress Cataloging-in-Publication Data
available upon request.**

ISBN 978-1-936096-15-2

Manufactured in China
1 3 5 7 9 10 8 6 4 2
First Edition

CONTENTS

INTRODUCTION

Eisaku Noro has been producing yarns for over forty years. His eponymous company located in Japan's Aichi province is known the world over for its extraordinary yarns, which are lovingly and carefully produced from the finest natural raw materials, including wool, silk, mohair and angora. Noro's commitment to ecologically sound manufacturing practices long predates the current trend. But the most remarkable feature of Noro yarns is their unique and striking color combinations. Eisaku Noro's artistic sensibility is apparent in the painterly palettes of his yarns, which are all hand colored. Each ball or hank passes through a spectrum of striking shades, whether serene, earthy hues or rich, saturated jewel tones. A single ball of yarn might progress from coral to amethyst to dove gray, or from seafoam green to chocolate brown, with blush pink accents along the way.

For *Knit Noro*, twenty-six top knitwear designers were invited to create knits that explore and expand the possibilities of these luxurious yarns. Working in *Kureyon*, *Silk Garden*, *Silk Garden Sock* and *Taiyo* yarns, they produced a collection of pullovers, cardigans, vests, tunics, shawls, scarves, hats, gloves, socks and afghans that dazzle the eye and will delight knitters of all skill levels. Theresa Schabes's belted cardigan vest shimmers in a range of ruby red hues. Mary Scott Huff's Fair Isle cardigan is a masterpiece of color and pattern. Colors go this way and that in Rosemary Drysdale's gorgeous entrelac scarf. Michele Wang's cowl neck tunic combines rich earth tones and several cable patterns to create incredible texture. Anna-Beth Meyer-Graham's modular afghan evokes an Impressionist painting of waterlilies. Tina Whitmore alternates two balls of a single colorway to create a charming felted cloche in a subtle striped pattern. These stunning yarns take classic shapes and stylish basics to another level, while innovative designs showcase Noro's avant-garde qualities. The result is a collection of wearable art, alive with color.

THE PROJECTS

Belted Cardigan Vest

Belted Cardigan Vest

Figure-flattering diagonal stripes and a waist-cinching belt create a silhouette that everyone can wear. This vest dazzles in rich shades of red.

Designed by Theresa Schabes

Skill Level: ■■■□

Materials

- 9 (10, 12, 14) 1¾oz/50g skeins (each approx 110yd/100m) of Noro *Silk Garden* (silk/kid mohair/wool) in #84
- Size 7 (4.5mm) needles
- Size 8 (5mm) circular needle, 24"/60cm or longer, OR SIZE TO OBTAIN GAUGE
- Stitch markers
- Tapestry needle

Sizes

Sized for Small (Medium, Large, X-Large)

Knitted Measurements

Bust (closed) 36 (41, 46, 52)"/91.5 (104, 117, 132)cm
Length 25 (26, 27, 28)"/ 63.5 (66, 68.5, 71)cm

Gauges

18 sts and 26 rows = 4"/10cm over reverse St st using larger needles.
18 sts and 32 rows = 4"/10cm over garter st using larger needles.
TAKE TIME TO CHECK GAUGES.

Stitch Glossary

Kfb K in front and back of st.
Pfb P in front and back of st.
W&T Wrap and turn.

Garter Stitch with Slip Stitch Edge

Row 1 Sl 1 wyib, k to end.
Rep row 1 for pattern.

Back

With larger needle, cast on 20 (23, 23, 26) sts. Work 144 (164, 184, 208) rows of garter st pat for 72 (82, 92, 104) ridges. Bind off, slipping the first st and leaving the last st on the needle. Rotate piece to work across the long edge. Pick up and k72 (82, 92, 104) sts in the "bumps" in front of the slipped sts—73 (83, 93, 105) sts. Mark the 37th (42nd, 47th, 53rd) stitch (center).
(**Note** The sl st edge of the pick-up will lie on the RS to form a decorative trim.)

Right side base triangle
Row 1 (RS) Pfb, p1, w&t.
Row 2 and all WS rows Knit.
Row 3 Pfb, p to wrapped st, lift wrap and p tog tbl with wrapped st, p1, w&t.
Rows 5 and 7 Pfb, p to wrapped st, lift wrap and p tog tbl with wrapped st, p2, w&t.
Rep rows 2–7 until there is 1 unworked st between last wrapped st and center st and ending with row 7 (5, 3, 7), then work row 2.
Next row (RS) Pfb, p to wrapped st, lift wrap and p tog tbl with wrapped st, p1—50 (57, 64, 72) sts. Break yarn.
Left side base triangle
With WS facing, slide markers and sts to right end of needle and attach yarn.

Row 1 (WS) Kfb, k1, w&t.

Row 2 and all RS rows Purl.

Row 3 Kfb, k to wrapped st, lift wrap and k tog with wrapped st, k1, w&t.

Rows 5 and 7 Kfb, k to wrapped st, lift wrap and k tog with wrapped st, k2, w&t.

Rep rows 2–7 until there is 1 st between last wrapped st and center st and ending with row 7 (5, 3, 7)—47 (54, 62, 69) sts on right-hand needle. Work row 2.

Full back

Joining row (WS) Kfb, k to wrapped st, lift wrap and k tog with wrapped st, sk2p, k to end—99 (113, 127, 143) sts.

Row 1 (RS) Purl.

Row 2 Kfb, k to 1 st before center st, sk2p, k to last st, kfb.

Rep rows 1 and 2 until side edge of back measures 25 (26, 27, 28)"/63.5 (66, 68.5, 71)cm from beg.

Shoulder and neck shaping

Row 1 (WS) Bind off 2 sts, k to 1 st before center st, sk2p, k to end.

Row 2 Bind off 2 sts, p to end.

Row 3 Bind off 3 sts, k to 1 st before center st, sk2p, k to end.

Row 4 Bind off 3 sts, p to end.

Row 5 Bind off 3 sts, k to 1 st before center st, sk2p, k to end.

Row 6 Bind off 3 sts, p to end.

Rep rows 1–6 until 33 (36, 39, 44) sts rem.

Next row (WS) Bind off 8 sts, k to 1 st before center st, sk2p, k to end.

Next row Bind off 8 sts, p to end.

Cont working rows 1–6 as est before the last 2 rows until 1 st remains. Fasten off.

Left Front

With larger needle, cast on 20 (23, 23, 26) sts. Work 54 (64, 74, 86) rows in garter st pat for 27 (32, 37, 43) ridges. Bind off, slipping the first st and leaving last st on the needle. Rotate piece to work across the long edge. Pick up and k27 (32, 37, 43) sts in the "bumps" in front of the slipped sts—28 (33, 38, 44) sts.

Foll all instructions for right side base triangle until there is 1 unworked st, ending with row 7 (5, 3, 7)—38 (45, 52, 60) sts total. Do not bind off. K 1 row.

Row 1 (RS) Pfb, p to last 2 sts, p2tog (lift wrap to add to p2tog on first row 1).

Row 2 Knit.

Rep rows 1 and 2 until front measures 17 (18, 18, 19)"/43 (45.5, 45.5, 48.5)cm from beg along front edge (left-hand edge with RS facing), ending with a RS row.

Neck and shoulder shaping

Dec row (WS) K2tog, k to end.

Rep dec row every 6th row 5 (8, 8, 8) times more—32 (36, 43, 57) sts.

AT THE SAME TIME, when side edge measures 25 (26, 27, 28)"/63.5 (66, 68.5, 71)cm from beg, decrease for shoulder as foll:

Row 1 (RS) Bind off 2 sts, p to last 2 sts, p2tog.

Row 2 and all WS rows Knit.

Row 3 Bind off 3 sts, p to last 2 sts, p2tog.

Row 5 Bind off 3 sts, p to last 2 sts, p2tog.

Row 6 Knit.

Rep rows 1–6 until 1 st remains, rep rows 1 and/or 3 when necessary. Fasten off.

Right Front

Work garter st band as for left front. Break yarn after picking up sts and slide all sts to begin triangle at other end. Join yarn and foll all instructions for left side base triangle with the exception of working rows 2–7 until there is 1 unworked st, ending with row 7 (5, 3, 7)—38 (45, 52, 60) sts. Work row 2.

Next row (WS) Kfb, k to wrapped st, lift wrap and k tog with wrapped st, k1.

Row 1 (RS) Purl.

Row 2 Kfb, k to last 2 sts, k2tog.

Rep rows 1 and 2 until front measures 17 (18, 18, 19)"/43 (45.5, 45.5, 48.5)cm from beg along front edge (right-hand edge with RS facing), ending with a WS row.

Neck and shoulder shaping

Dec row (RS) P2tog, p to end.

Rep dec row every 6th row 5 (8, 8, 8) times more—32 (36, 43, 51) sts.

AT THE SAME TIME, when side edge measures 25 (26, 27, 28)"/63.5 (66, 68.5, 71)cm from beg, decrease for shoulder as foll:

Row 1 (WS) Bind off 2 sts, k to last 2 sts, k2tog.

Row 2 and all RS rows Purl.

Row 3 Bind off 3 sts, k to last 2 sts, k2tog.

Row 5 Bind off 3 sts, k to last 2 sts, k2tog.

Row 6 Knit.

Rep rows 1–6 until 1 st remains, working rows 1 and/or 3 when necessary. Fasten off.

Finishing

Block pieces to measurements. Sew shoulder seams.

Armbands

Place markers at each side edge 8 (8½, 9, 9½)"/20.5 (21.5, 23, 24)cm below shoulder seams. (Continued on page 136.)

Ridged Ripples Scarf

Ridged Ripples Scarf

A series of increases and decreases creates a beautiful faux cable effect in this double-sided neck warmer.

Designed by Tina Whitmore

Skill Level: ■■■□

Materials

■ 3 3½oz/100g balls (each approx 330 yd/300m) of Noro Yarns *Silk Garden Sock Yarn* (lamb's wool/silk/nylon/mohair) in #268
■ One size 7 (4.5mm) circular needle, 16"/40cm long, OR SIZE TO OBTAIN GAUGE

Knitted Measurements

Approx 4½" x 76"/11.5cm x 193cm

Gauge

33 sts and 23½ rows = 4"/10cm over St Pat using size 7 (4.5mm) circular needle. TAKE TIME TO CHECK GAUGE.

Notes

1) Scarf is worked in two halves from cast-on edge to center; each half is worked circularly and the two halves are joined using 3-needle bind-off.
2) Use two separate balls of yarn throughout. Designate one ball as Main Color (MC) and one ball as Contrast Color (CC). For the greatest color contrast and to make the stitch pattern stand out, start each ball of yarn at a different point in the color sequence from the other.
3) "Color dominance" is when one color seems more prominent than the other. To ensure consistency in color dominance, always strand MC (the dominant yarn) below CC (the non-dominant yarn), and CC above MC.

Stitch Glossary

Right Lifted Inc (RLI) Insert RH needle into top of st in row below next st on LH needle and knit this st.
Left Lifted Inc (LLI) Insert LH needle from back to front into st 2 rows below st on RH needle and knit this st.

Scarf

With MC, cast on 37 sts, place marker (pm), cast on another 37 sts, pm and join—74 sts.
Beg st pat
Rnd 1 *[K1MC, k1CC] 18 times, k1MC; rep from * once more.
Rnd 2 *[K1MC, k1CC] 4 times, k1MC, k2tog MC, [k1CC, k1MC] 3 times, k1CC, LLI with CC, k1MC, RLI with CC, k1CC, [k1MC, k1CC] 3 times, ssk MC, k1MC, [k1CC, k1MC] 4 times; rep from * once more.
Rnd 3 *[K1MC, k1CC] 4 times, k2tog MC, [k1CC, k1MC] 3 times, k1CC, LLI with MC, k1CC, k1MC, k1CC, RLI with MC, k1CC, [k1MC, k1CC] 3 times, ssk MC, [k1CC, k1MC] 4 times; rep from * once more.
Rnd 4 *[K1MC, k1CC] 3 times, k1MC, k2tog MC, [k1CC, k1MC] 3 times, k1CC, LLI with CC, [k1MC, k1CC] twice, k1MC, RLI with CC, k1CC, [k1MC, k1CC] 3 times, ssk MC, k1MC, [k1CC, k1MC] 3 times; rep from * once more.

Rnd 5 *[K1MC, k1CC] 3 times, k2tog MC, [k1CC, k1MC] 3 times, k1CC, LLI with MC, [k1CC, k1MC] 3 times, k1CC, RLI with MC, k1CC, [k1MC, k1CC] 3 times, ssk MC, [k1CC, k1MC] 3 times; rep from * once more.

Rnd 6 *[K1MC, k1CC] twice, k1MC, k2tog MC, [k1CC, k1MC] 3 times, k1CC, LLI with CC, [k1MC, k1CC] 4 times, k1MC, RLI with CC, k1CC, [k1MC, k1CC] 3 times, ssk MC, k1MC, [k1CC, k1MC] twice; rep from * once more.

Rnd 7 *[K1MC, k1CC] twice, k2tog MC, [k1CC, k1MC] 3 times, k1CC, LLI with MC, [k1CC, k1MC] 5 times, k1CC, RLI with MC, k1CC, [k1MC, k1CC] 3 times, ssk MC, [k1CC, k1MC] twice; rep from * once more.

Rnd 8 *K1MC, k1CC, k1MC, k2tog MC, [k1CC, k1MC] 3 times, k1CC, LLI with CC, [k1MC, k1CC] 6 times, k1MC, RLI with CC, k1CC, [k1MC, k1CC] 3 times, ssk MC, k1MC, k1CC, k1MC; rep from * once more.

Rnd 9 *K1MC, k1CC, k2tog MC, [k1CC, k1MC] 3 times, k1CC, LLI with MC, [k1CC, k1MC] 7 times, k1CC, RLI with MC, k1CC, [k1MC, k1CC] 3 times, ssk MC, k1CC, k1MC; rep from * once more.

Rnd 10 *K1MC, k2tog MC, [k1CC, k1MC] 3 times, k1CC, LLI with CC, [k1MC, k1CC] 8 times, k1MC, RLI with CC, k1CC, [k1MC, k1CC] 3 times, ssk MC, k1MC; rep from * once more.

Rnd 11 *K2tog MC, [k1CC, k1MC] 3 times, k1CC, LLI with MC, [k1CC, k1MC] 9 times, k1CC, RLI with MC, k1CC, [k1MC, k1CC] 3 times, ssk MC; rep from * once more.

Rnds 12–14 Rep rnd 1.

Rep rnds 1–14 fourteen times more, then work rnds 1–13 once more. Place sts on spare circular needle. Break yarns. Work 2nd half of scarf as for first. Break yarns, leaving a long tail of CC for 3-needle bind-off. Turn 2nd half of scarf inside out.

Place first scarf half inside the 2nd half, with RS tog. Align needles so that working ends are tog.

With CC from outer tube, join sts on needles, using 3-needle bind-off.

Finishing

Block piece. Weave in ends. Turn scarf RS out. Seam open ends of scarf closed. ∎

Fair Isle Cardigan

Fair Isle Cardigan

Contrasting shades of *Silk Garden Sock Yarn* knit in a Fair Isle pattern create a stunning tapestry-like effect. Corrugated ribbing frames the intricate design.

Designed by Mary Scott Huff

Skill Level: ■■■■

Materials

- 4 (4, 4, 4, 5, 5) 3½oz/100g skeins (each approx 330 yd/300m) of Noro *Silk Garden Sock* (wool/silk/nylon/mohair) in #269 (A)
- 3 (3, 4, 4, 5, 5) skeins in color #324 (B)
- Size 1 (2.25mm) circular needles, 29"/72cm, 24"/60cm and 16"/40cm long
- Size 2 (3mm) circular needles, 29"/72cm, 24"/60cm and 16"/40cm long, OR SIZE TO OBTAIN GAUGE
- 2½yd/2.5m 1"/2.5cm grosgrain ribbon
- Nine ½"/12mm buttons
- Sewing needle and matching thread
- Tapestry needle
- Stitch markers
- Stitch holders or waste yarn

Sizes

Sized for X-Small (Small, Medium, Large, X-Large, XX-Large).

Knitted Measurements

Bust 36 (38¼, 40½, 45, 49½, 54)"/91.5 (97, 103, 114.5, 125.5, 137)cm
Length 21½ (22, 22½, 23, 23½, 24)"/54.5 (56, 57, 58.5, 59.5, 61)cm

Gauge

32 sts and 36 rows = 4"/10cm over chart pat using larger needles. TAKE TIME TO CHECK GAUGE.

Corrugated Rib

(over an even number of sts)
Row 1 *K1 with A, p1 with B; rep from *, stranding unused color loosely on WS.
Row 2 *K1 with B, p 1 with A; rep from *.
Rep rows 1 and 2 for pattern when working back and forth.
Rep row 1 only when working in the round.

Body

With smaller circular needle and A, cast on 288 (306, 324, 360, 396, 432) sts. Work back and forth in corrugated rib for 5"/12.5cm, ending with a WS row. Pm, cast on 6 steek sts, pm, and join for working in the round. Change to larger needle and work rnds 1–48 of chart, working steek sts in alternating colors throughout. Repeat rnds 49–66 of chart until piece measures 17¾ (18, 18¼, 18½, 18¾, 19)"/45 (45.5, 46.5, 47, 47.5, 48)cm from beg.
Shape neckline
Bind off 6 steek sts, work 31 (33, 33, 35, 37, 37) sts and place on holder, k to end of rnd, and place last 31 (33, 33, 35, 37, 37) sts on holder—226 (240, 258, 290, 322, 358) sts. Pm, cast on 6 new steek sts, pm, and rejoin for working in the round. Work even in pat for 3¾ (4, 4¼, 4½, 4¾, 5)"/9.5 (10, 11, 11.5, 12, 12.5)cm.
Bind off 6 steek sts and place sts on holders as foll: 37 (39, 44, 51, 58, 67) sts for left front shoulder. Bind off 6 sts (this is where you will cut the left armhole). 36 (39, 43, 50, 57, 66) sts for left back shoulder. 68 (72, 72, 76, 80, 80) sts for back neck, 36 (39, 43, 50, 57, 66) sts for right back shoulder. Bind off 6 sts (this is where you will cut the right armhole). 37 (39, 44, 51, 58, 67) sts for right front shoulder. Machine-stitch to secure sts and cut center front steeks. Block body.

Sleeves

(work both sleeves simultaneously)
With smaller needle, cast on 70 (72, 72, 74, 78, 82) sts. Work back

and forth in k1, p1 corrugated rib for 1"/2.5cm, ending with a WS row. Break yarn and place all sts on a holder. Make 2nd cuff to match, matching color repeats in first cuff, and ending with a WS row.

Join sleeves

Work 70 (72, 72, 74, 78, 82) sts of 2nd cuff, pm, cast on 6 steek sts, pm. Work sts of first cuff from holder onto the same needle, pm, cast on 6 steek sts, pm. Join for working in the round—70 (72, 72, 74, 78, 82) sts for each cuff, with 6 steek sts between each. Change to larger needle. Starting with stitch 2 (1, 1, 18, 16, 14) and ending with stitch 17 (18, 18, 1, 3, 5), work chart rows 1–48 on each sleeve, centering pat motifs. AT THE SAME TIME, increase 1 st each side of each sleeve, every 5th (5th, 5th, 4th, 4th, 3rd) rnd 25 (26, 28, 33, 35, 40) times. Repeat rows 49–66 on both sleeves, continuing increases as established—120 (124, 128, 140, 148, 162) sts each sleeve excluding steek sts. Work even until sleeves measures 19 (20, 19½, 19, 18½, 17)"/48.5 (51, 49.5, 48.5, 47, 43)cm from beg. Bind off both sets of 6 steek sts and place each set of sleeve sts on waste yarn. Machine stitch to secure sts and cut steeks, separating sleeves. Block pieces.

Sleeve finishing

Sew sleeve seams from the RS using tapestry needle and yarn. Cover cut steek edges on WS with grosgrain ribbon, sewing invisibly by hand. Starting at seam with RS facing, place sleeve sts on needle and p 7 rnds for sleeve facing, increasing 1 st at beg and end of every rnd—134 (138, 142, 154, 162, 176) sts. Bind off loosely. Repeat finishing for second sleeve.

Finishing

Measure completed sleeve tops (below facing). Measure this same distance down from bound-off steek sts at top of body tube for armhole steeks. Mark cutting line with contrasting waste yarn. Machine-stitch to secure sts and cut armhole opening. Repeat for second armhole. Join shoulder seams using 3-needle bind-off.

Neckline finishing

With RS facing and smaller needle, pick up and k31 (33, 33, 35, 37, 37) held right front neck sts, 28 (30, 31, 33, 35, 37) sts along right steek edge, 68 (72, 72, 76, 80, 80) live back neck sts, 28 (30, 31, 33, 35, 37) sts along left steek edge, 31 (33, 33, 35, 37, 37) held left front neck sts—186 (198, 200, 212, 224, 228) sts. Work back and forth in k1, p1 corrugated rib for 1"/2.5cm. Work miters at inside front corners by decreasing 2 sts at each corner every RS row. Bind off neck edging. Cover cut steek sts on WS with grosgrain ribbon, sewing invisibly by hand.

Button band

With RS facing, pick up and k143 (145, 147, 149, 151, 153) sts along left front edge. Beg with k1, work back and forth in corrugated rib for 1"/2.5cm. Bind off loosely.

Buttonhole band

With RS facing, pick up and k143 (145, 147, 149, 151, 153) sts along right front edge. Beg with k1, work back and forth in corrugated rib for ½"/1.5cm, ending with a WS row.

Buttonhole row (RS) Work 9 sts, k2tog, cast on 2 sts (one of each color), ssk, [work 13 (14, 14, 14, 14, 15) sts, k2tog, cast on 2 sts (one of each color), ssk] 8 times, work to end of row.

Continue in corrugated rib until band measures 1"/2.5cm. Bind off loosely. Cover cut steek edges on WS with grosgrain ribbon, sewing invisibly by hand. Sew buttons to button band to correspond with buttonholes. ■ *(Chart on page 137.)*

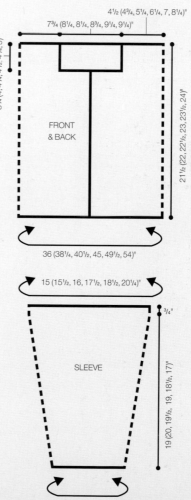

4½ (4¾, 5¼, 6¼, 7, 8¼)"

7¾ (8¼, 8¼, 8¾, 9¼, 9¼)"

3¾ (4, 4¼, 4½, 4¾, 5)"

FRONT & BACK

21½ (22, 22½, 23, 23½, 24)"

36 (38¼, 40½, 45, 49½, 54)"

15 (15½, 16, 17½, 18½, 20¼)"

¾"

SLEEVE

19 (20, 19½, 19, 18½, 17)"

8¾ (9, 9, 9¼, 9¾, 10¼)"

Cabled Cap

Cabled Cap

The gorgeous colors of *Silk Garden* are highlighted in a series of textured stitch patterns that begins with a cabled rib then flows into a zigzag pattern and finishes in a rib stitch.

Designed by Faina Goberstein

Skill Level: ◼◼◼☐

Materials

- 2 1¾oz/50g balls (each approx 110 yd/100m) of Noro Yarns *Silk Garden* (silk/mohair/lamb's wool) in #325
- One each sizes 6 and 8 (4mm and 5mm) circular needle, 16"/40cm long, OR SIZE TO OBTAIN GAUGE
- One set (5) size 8 (5mm) double-pointed needles (dpn)
- Stitch marker
- Cable needle (cn)

Knitted Measurements

Band circumference 21"/53.5cm
Depth 8¾"/ 22cm

Gauge

21 sts and 30 rows = 4"/10cm over zigzag pat using larger needle. TAKE TIME TO CHECK GAUGE.

Stitch Glossary

2-st LT With RH needle behind LH needle, k 2nd st on LH needle through back loop, then k first st on LH needle through front loop, sl both sts from needle.
3-st RC Sl 2 sts to cn and hold to *back*, k1, k2 from cn.
3-st LC Sl 1 st to cn and hold to *front*, k2, k1 from cn.

Cabled Rib

(over a multiple of 4 sts)
Rnds 1 and 2 *K2, p2; rep from * around.
Rnd 3 *2-st LT, p2; rep from * around.
Rnd 4 Rep rnd 1.
Rep rnds 1–4 for cabled rib.

Zigzag Pattern

(over a multiple of 3 sts)
Rnds 1 and 2 *Sl 1 purlwise wyib, k2; rep from * around.
Rnd 3 *3-st LC; rep from * around.
Rnd 4 Knit.
Rnd 5 *Yo, k2tog, k1; rep from * around.
Rnd 6 Knit.
Rnds 7 and 8 *K2, sl 1 purlwise wyib; rep from * around.
Rnd 9 *3-st RC; rep from * around.
Rnd 10 Knit.
Rep rnds 1–10 for zigzag pat.

Hat

With smaller circular needle, cast on 112 sts. Pm and join, being careful not to twist sts. Work in cabled rib for 14 rnds, ending with rnd 2. Change to larger circular needle.
Inc rnd [K8, M1] 14 times—126 sts.
Work zigzag pat for 30 rnds.
Beg rib
Rnds 1–6 *K1, p2; rep from * around. Piece measures approx 6¾"/17cm from beg.

Crown shaping

(**Note** Change to dpns when work becomes too tight to fit on circular needle.)

Rnd 1 *K1, p2tog; rep from * around—84 sts.

Rnds 2–5 *K1, p1; rep from * around.

Rnd 6 *Ssk; rep from * around—42 sts.

Rnd 7 Knit.

Rnd 8 *K2tog; rep from * around—21 sts.

Rnd 9 Knit.

Rnd 10 *K2tog; rep from * to last st, k1—11 sts.

Cut yarn and use darning needle to slide tail through all rem sts. Pull tight and fasten securely.

Finishing

Weave in loose ends.

Block with steam lightly. Gather cabled rib band and let it dry well. ■

Chevron Throw

Chevron Throw

Oversized strips are knit on the bias to create a diagonal-stripe effect. The strips are then joined to form a dramatic chevron pattern.

Designed by Grace Akhrem

Skill Level: ■■□□

Materials

- 12 1¾oz/50g balls (each approx 110yd/100m) of Noro *Kureyon* (wool) in #252
- One pair size 8 (5mm) needles OR SIZE TO OBTAIN GAUGE
- One size 8 (5mm) circular needle, 40"/101cm long
- 1 small hank of embroidery floss

Knitted Measurements

35" x 45½"/89cm x 115.5cm

Gauge

14 sts and 28 rows = 4"/10cm over garter st, lightly blocked, using size 8 (5mm) needles.
TAKE TIME TO CHECK GAUGE.

Notes

1) Sl sts purlwise with yarn in front (then bring yarn to back of work again).
2) For ease of working, mark RS of work.

Throw

Strips (make 5)

Cast on 1 st.

Corner inc section

Row 1 (RS) [K into front, back and front] of st—3 sts.

Row 2 (WS) Sl 1, k2.

Row 3 Sl 1, [M1, k1] twice—5 sts.

Row 4 Sl 1, k to end.

Row 5 Sl 1, M1, k to last st, M1, k1—7 sts.

[Rep rows 4 and 5] 19 times more—45 sts.

Next row (WS) Rep row 4.

Bias knit section

Row 1 (RS) Sl 1, M1, k to last 3 sts, k2tog, k1.

Row 2 Sl 1, k to end.

Rep rows 1 and 2 until piece measures approx 32"/81cm from beg (measured along right-hand edge).

Corner dec section

Row 1 (RS) Sl 1, ssk, k to last 3 sts, k2tog, k1—43 sts.

Row 2 Sl 1, k to end.

[Rep rows 1 and 2] 19 times more—5 sts.

Next row (RS) Sl 1, SK2P, k1—3 sts.

Next row Sl 1, k2.

Next row SK2P. Fasten off last st.

Finishing

Weave in all loose ends and lightly block all pieces. Using the embroidery floss and mattress st, seam long edges of strips to each other, alternating direction of garter ridges from one strip to the next to form chevrons (see photo).

Border

With RS facing and circular needle, pick up and k111 sts along one long edge.

Rows 1–11 Sl 1, k to end. Bind off all sts.

Rep for other long edge.

Work in same way along both shorter edges, picking up 94 sts. ∎

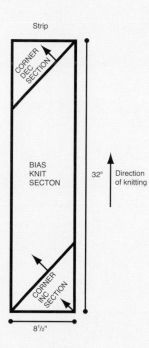

Strip

CORNER DEC SECTION

BIAS KNIT SECTON

32"

↑ Direction of knitting

CORNER INC SECTION

8¹/₂"

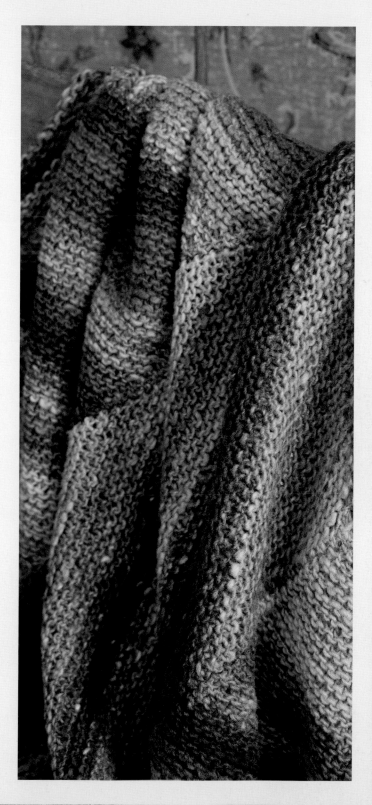

Entrelac Scarf

Entrelac Scarf

Entrelac, a technique that creates a woven effect, shows off the dazzling colors of *Kureyon* beautifully.

Designed by Rosemary Drysdale

Skill Level: ■■■□

Materials

- 4 1¾oz/50g balls (each approx 110 yd/100m) of Noro Yarns *Kureyon* (wool) in #102
- One pair size 7 (4.5mm) needles, OR SIZE TO OBTAIN GAUGE

Knitted Measurements

Approx 8" x 56"/20.5cm x 142cm

Gauges

16 sts and 20 rows = 4"/10cm over St st using size 7 (4.5mm) needles.
One 8-st x 16-row rectangle measures 1¾" x 2"/4.5cm x 5cm.
TAKE TIME TO CHECK GAUGES.

Pattern Stitch

(over 8 sts)
Row 1 (RS) K4, p1, k3.
Row 2 (WS) K1, p1, k3, p1, k2.
Rep rows 1 and 2 for pat st.

Notes

1) Turn work after every row unless indicated otherwise.
2) Use cable cast-on throughout.

Scarf

Tier 1
*Cast on 8 sts. Work in pat st for 16 rows. Do *not* break yarn. Rep from * twice more (3 rectangles made).

Tier 2
Bind off from first rectangle 7 sts purlwise—1 st rem on RH needle. Do *not* turn. With RS facing, pick up and k7 sts along left edge of rectangle—8 sts. *Sl last picked-up st to LH needle, ssk, turn.
Row 1 (WS) K1, p1, k3, p1, k2.
Row 2 (RS) K4, p1, k2, ssk. Rep rows 1 and 2 six times more. Do *not* turn after last row. With RS facing, pick up and k8 sts along left edge of next rectangle.
Rep from * once more. Do *not* turn after last row. With RS facing, pick up and k8 sts along left edge of next rectangle.
Beg with row 2, work pat st for 14 rows, ending with row 1.

Tier 3
Bind off from first rectangle 7 sts knitwise—1 st rem on RH needle. Do *not* turn. With WS facing, pick up and p7 sts along left edge of rectangle—8 sts. *Sl last picked-up st to LH needle, ssk, turn.
Row 1 (RS) K4, p1, k3.
Row 2 (WS) K1, p1, k3, p1, k1, ssk.
Rep rows 1 and 2 six times more. Do *not* turn after last row. With WS facing, pick up and p8 sts along left edge of next rectangle.
Rep from * once more. Do *not* turn after last row. With WS facing, pick up and p8 sts along left edge of next rectangle.
Beg with row 1, work pat st for 14 rows, ending with row 2.
[Rep Tiers 2 and 3] 20 times more.

Last Tier
Work as for Tier 2, except bind off the last row of each rectangle purlwise, and pick up and k7 sts for each rectangle. Fasten off last st.

Finishing

Weave in ends. Block to measurements. ■

Long Vest

Long Vest

This stunning ultra-long vest has a bias-knit bodice and lacy shell-pattern skirt, resulting in multi-directional stripes.

Designed by Dana Matuskey

Skill Level: ■■■☐

Materials

- 11 (13, 15) 1¾oz/50g skeins (each approx 110 yd/100m) of Noro *Silk Garden* (silk/kid mohair/wool) in #325
- Size 7 (4.5mm) needles OR SIZE TO OBTAIN GAUGE
- Size 8 (5mm) needles OR SIZE TO OBTAIN GAUGE
- Stitch markers
- Tapestry needle

Sizes
Sized for Small (Medium, Large)

Knitted Measurements
Bust 34 (37½, 41)"/86.5 (95, 104)cm
Length 36 (37, 38½)"/91.5 (94, 98)cm

Gauges
20 sts and 12 rows = 4¾" x 2"/12 x 5cm over shell pattern (excluding garter ridge) using larger needles
19 sts and 38 rows = 4"/10cm over garter st using smaller needles
TAKE TIME TO CHECK GAUGES.

Shell Pattern (for gauge)
With larger needles, cast on 20 sts. K 3 rows.
Row 1 (RS) K2, yo, pm, [k1, p2] 5 times, k1, pm, yo, k2—22 sts.
Row 2 K3, [p1, k2] 5 times, p1, k3.
Row 3 K3, yo, [k1, p2] 5 times, k1, yo, k3—24 sts.
Row 4 K4, [p1, k2] 5 times, p1, k4.
Row 5 K4, yo, [k1, p2] 5 times, k1, yo, k4—26 sts.
Row 6 K5, [p1, k2] 5 times, p1, k5.
Row 7 K5, yo, [k1, p2] 5 times, k1, yo, k5—28 sts.
Row 8 K6, [p1, k2] 5 times, p1, k6.
Row 9 K6, yo, [k1, p2] 5 times, k1, yo, k6—30 sts.
Row 10 K7, [p2, k1] 5 times, p1, k7.
Row 11 K7, yo, [k1, p2] 5 times, k1, yo, k7—32 sts.
Row 12 K7, [sk2p] 6 times, k7—20 sts.

Note
Garment back is worked in 2 sections, right and left sides.

Left Front and Right Back (make 2)
Lower section—shell pattern
With larger needles, cast on 40 (44, 48) sts loosely. K 5 rows.
Row 1 (RS) *K2 (3, 4), yo, [k1, p2] 5 times, k1, yo, k2 (3, 4); rep from * to end—44 (48, 52) sts.
Row 2 *K3 (4, 5), [p1, k2] 5 times, p1, k3 (4, 5); rep from * to end.
Row 3 *K3 (4, 5), yo, [k1, p2] 5 times, k1, yo, k3 (4, 5); rep from * to end—48 (52, 56) sts.
Row 4 *K4 (5, 6), [p1, k2] 5 times, p1, k4 (5, 6); rep from * to end.
Row 5 * K4 (5, 6), yo, [k1, p2] 5 times, k1, yo, k4 (5, 6); rep from * to end—52 (56, 60) sts.
Row 6 *K5 (6, 7), [p1, k2] 5 times, p1, k5 (6, 7); rep from * to end.
Row 7 *K5 (6, 7), yo, [k1, p2] 5 times, k1, yo, k5 (6, 7); rep from * to end—56 (60, 64) sts.

Row 8 *K6 (7, 8), [p1, k2] 5 times, p1, k6 (7, 8); rep from * to end.

Row 9 *K6 (7, 8), yo, [k1, p2] 5 times, k1, yo, k6 (7, 8); rep from * to end—60 (64, 68) sts.

Row 10 *K7 (8, 9), [p1, k2] 5 times, p1, k7 (8, 9); rep from * to end.

Row 11 *K7 (8, 9), yo, [k1, p2] 5 times, k1, yo, k7 (8, 9); rep from * to end—64 (68, 72) sts.

Row 12 K7 (8, 9), [SK2P] 6 times, k14, [SK2P] 6 times, k7 (8, 9)—40 (44, 48) sts.

Repeat rows 1–12 ten times more. Piece measures approx 21"/53.5cm.

Upper section

Change to smaller needles.

Size S dec row (RS) [K3, k2tog] 4 times, [k2tog, k3] 4 times—32 sts.

Size M dec row (RS) K3, k2tog, k2, k2tog, [k3, k2tog] twice, [k2, k2tog] twice, [k3, k2tog] twice, k2, k2tog, k3—35 sts.

Size L dec row (RS) *[K3, k2tog] twice, k2, [k2tog, k3] twice, [k2tog] twice, [k3, k2tog] twice, k2, [k2tog, k3] twice—38 sts. K 3 rows.

**Diagonal section

Row 1 (RS) Kfb, k1; turn.

Row 2 Sl 1 knitwise, k2; turn.

Row 3 [Kfb] twice, ssk; turn.

Row 4 Sl 1 knitwise, k4; turn.

Row 5 Kfb, k2, kfb, ssk; turn.

Row 6 Sl 1 knitwise, k6; turn.

Row 7 Kfb, k to 2 sts before gap, kfb, ssk; turn.

Row 8 Sl 1 knitwise, k to end.

Rep rows 7 and 8 until there are 10 (11, 12) unworked sts, ending with a WS row.

Armhole shaping

Row 1 (RS) K2tog, k to 2 sts before gap, kfb, ssk; turn.

Row 2 Sl 1 knitwise, k to end.

Rows 3–8 (3–10, 3–12) Rep rows 1 and 2.

Row 9 (11, 13) K to 2 sts before gap, kfb, ssk; turn.

Row 10 (12, 14) Sl 1 knitwise, k to end.

Rows 11–16 (13–18, 15–20) Rep last 2 rows (2 unworked sts after row 16 [18, 20]).

Row 17 (19, 21) Kfb, k to 1 st before gap, sk2p.

Row 18 (20, 22) Knit.

Row 19 (21, 23) Kfb, k to last 2 sts, ssk.

Row 20 (20, 24) Knit.

Rep last 2 rows until armhole measures 7½ (8, 9)"/19 (20.5, 23)cm.

Shape shoulder

Next row (RS) K2tog, k to last 2 sts, ssk.

Rep last row every RS row until 4 sts rem, ending with a WS row.

Last row (RS) [K2tog] twice, pass first st over 2nd st. Fasten off.**

Right Front and Left Back (make 2)

Work lower section same as for left front/right back.

Upper section

Change to smaller needles.

Size S dec row (RS) [K3, k2tog] 4 times, [k2tog, k3] 4 times—32 sts.

Size M dec row (RS) K3, k2tog, k2, k2tog, [k3, k2tog] twice, [k2, k2tog] twice, [k3, k2tog] twice, k2, k2tog, k3—35 sts.

Size L dec row (RS) *[K3, k2tog] twice, k2, [k2tog, K3] twice, [K2tog] twice, [k3, k2tog] twice, K2, [K2tog, K3] twice—38 sts. K 4 rows.

Starting with row 1, cont same as for left front and right back from ** to **, except that odd-numbered rows are WS rows and even-numbered rows are RS rows.

Finishing

Sew center seam of Left and Right backs. Sew 4¼ (4½, 5"/11 (11.5, 12.5)cm shoulder seams. Sew side seams from the armhole down, leaving the last 3 shells open. Tack down corners of lapels. ■

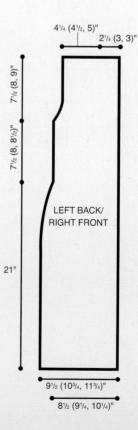

4¼ (4½, 5)"
2¼ (3, 3)"
7½ (8, 9)"
7½ (8, 8½)"
LEFT BACK/
RIGHT FRONT
21"
9½ (10¾, 11¾)"
8½ (9¼, 10¼)"

Diamonds and Stripes Gloves

Diamonds and Stripes Gloves

Knitting with a variegated yarn like *Silk Garden Sock Yarn* infuses a simple colorwork pattern with complexity, as seen in these elegant gloves.

Designed by Cheryl Murray

Skill Level: ■■■■

Materials

- 1 3½oz/100g ball (each approx 330 yd/300m) of Noro *Silk Garden Sock Yarn* (lamb's wool/silk/nylon/mohair) in #252 (MC) and #272 (CC)
- One set (4) size 3 (3.25mm) double-pointed needles (dpns) OR SIZE TO OBTAIN GAUGE
- Stitch markers and holders
- Yarn needle

Knitted Measurements

Hand circumference 7¾"/19.5cm
Length 10"/25.5cm

Gauge

28 sts and 36 rnds = 4"/10cm over Hand Chart using size 3 (3.25mm) needles. TAKE TIME TO CHECK GAUGE.

Stripe Pattern

Rnds 1 and 2 Work in pat with MC.
Rnds 3 and 4 Work in pat with CC.
Rep rnds 1–4 for stripe pat.

Left Glove

With MC, cast on 52 sts and divide over 3 dpns. Place marker (pm) and join, being careful not to twist.

Cuff

Work in k2, p2 rib and stripe pat for 26 rnds, inc 3 sts evenly around on last rnd—55 sts. Cuff measures approx 2½"/6.5cm from beg. Cont in St st (k every rnd) as foll:

Beg charts

Rnd 1 Work 1 st of Gusset Chart, pm, work 6-st rep of Hand Chart to end. Cont in pats as established, working Gusset Chart between markers, through rnd 23 of Gusset Chart—19 sts between markers.

Next rnd Slip rnd marker to RH needle, place 19 gusset sts on a holder, remove 2nd marker and work Hand Chart as established to end of rnd—54 sts. Work even until 8 rnds of Hand Chart have been worked a total of 4 times from beg, then work rnds 1–3 once more. Hand measures approx 4" above cuff.

Little Finger

With MC, k21 and place these sts on a holder for back of hand, arrange next 12 sts over 3 dpns, placing last 21 sts of rnd on 2nd holder for palm. With MC, cast on 2 sts—14 sts. Pm and k 2 rnds with MC. Cont in stripe pat as established for 19 rnds more, ending with 1 rnd MC.

Shape top: Next rnd With MC, [k5, k2tog] twice—12 sts.
Next rnd With CC, knit.
Next rnd With CC, [k1, k2tog] 4 times—8 sts. Cut yarns, pull tails through rem sts and tighten to close. Finger measures approx 2¾"/7cm from base.

Ring Finger

Divide rem 42 sts over 3 dpns. Next rnd with MC, pick up and k2 sts from base of little finger, pm, k to end of rnd—44 sts. Join CC and k7 from palm, place next 14 palm sts and 14 back-of-hand sts on a holder, with CC, k7 back-of-hand sts, k2 from base of little finger—16 sts. Cont in stripe pat as established for 26 more rnds, ending with 1 rnd MC.

Shape top: Next rnd with MC, [k2, k2tog] 4 times—12 sts.

Next rnd With CC, knit.

Next rnd With CC, [k1, k2tog] 4 times—8 sts. Cut yarns, pull tails through rem sts and tighten to close. Finger measures approx 3¼"/8cm from base.

Middle Finger

Arrange 7 palm sts and 7 back-of-hand sts on 3 dpns. With CC, pick up and k2 sts from base of ring finger, pm, k to end of rnd—16 sts. Cont in stripe pat as established for 28 rnds more, ending with 1 rnd CC.

Shape top: Next rnd With CC, [k2, k2tog] 4 times—12 sts.

Next rnd With MC, knit.

Next rnd With MC, [k1, k2tog] 4 times 8 sts. Cut yarns, pull tails through rem sts and tighten to close. Finger measures approx 3½"/9cm from base.

Index Finger

Arrange rem 14 sts on 3 dpns. With CC, pick up and k2 sts from base of middle finger, pm, k to end of rnd—16 sts. Complete as for ring finger.

Thumb

Arrange 19 sts on 3 dpns. With MC, pick up and k2 sts from base of thumb, pm, k to end of rnd—21 sts. Cont in stripe pat as established for 18 rnds more, ending with 1 rnd CC.

Shape top: Next rnd With CC, [k1, k2tog] 7 times—14 sts.

Next rnd With MC, knit.

Next rnd With MC, [k2tog] 7 times—7 sts. Cut yarns, pull tails through rem sts and tighten to close. Thumb measures approx 2½"/6.5cm from base.

Right Glove

Work as for left glove (reversing palm and back-of-hand designations).

Finishing

Weave in ends, using tails to close any gaps that might occur at base of fingers or thumb. ■

Gusset Chart

Key
- Knit with MC
- Knit with CC
- M Make 1 with MC

Hand Chart

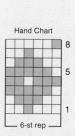

6-st rep

Reversible Cabled Scarf

Reversible Cabled Scarf

The vibrant shades of *Taiyo* are showcased to great effect in this stunning double-sided scarf.

Designed by Grace Akhrem

Skill Level: ■■□□

Materials

- 3 3½oz/100g balls (each approx 220 yd/200m) of Noro *Taiyo* (cotton/silk/wool/nylon) in #6
- One pair size 10 (6mm) knitting needles
OR SIZE TO OBTAIN GAUGE
- Cable needle (cn)

Knitted Measurements

Approx 6" x 95¾"/15 x 243cm

Gauge

27 sts and 18 rows = 4"/10cm over cable pat using size 10 (6mm) needles.
TAKE TIME TO CHECK GAUGE.

Stitch Glossary

8-st LC Sl 4 sts to cn and hold to *front*, [k1, p1] twice, then [k1, p1] twice from cn.

Scarf

Cast on 40 sts.

Beg cable pat

(**Note** Sl sts purlwise with yarn in front.)

Rows 1–5 Sl 1, *p1, k1; rep from * to last st, k1.

Row 6 (RS) Sl 1, p1, [k1, p1] 3 times, 8-st LC, [k1, p1] 4 times, 8-st LC, [k1, p1] 3 times, k2.

Rows 7–11 Rep rows 1–5.

Row 12 *8-st LC, [k1, p1] 4 times; rep from * once more, 8-st LC.

Rep rows 1–12 thirty-four times more. Rep rows 1–11 once more. Bind off all sts.

Finishing

Weave in all loose ends and block lightly. ■

Spiral Beanie

Spiral Beanie

A lovely lace pattern that creates a spiral effect, combined with the sumptuous shades of *Silk Garden*, transforms a simple beanie shape into a work of art.

Designed by Linda Medina

Skill Level: ■■■□

Materials
- 2 1¾oz/50g balls (each approx 110 yd/100m) of Noro *Silk Garden* (silk/mohair/wool) in #307
- One size 7 (4.5mm) circular needle, 16"/40cm long, OR SIZE TO OBTAIN GAUGE
- One set (5) size 7 (4.5mm) double-pointed needles (dpns)
- Stitch marker
- Yarn needle

Knitted Measurements
Circumference 20"/51cm
Length 8"/20.5cm

Gauge
24 sts and 27 rnds = 4"/10cm over 4-rnd rep of chart pat, using size 7 (4.5mm) needle. TAKE TIME TO CHECK GAUGE.

Hat
With circular needle, cast on 120 sts. Place marker and join, being careful not to twist sts. Work in k1, p1 ribbing for 1¼"/3cm.
Work rnds 1–4 of chart pat 8 times.
Crown shaping
(**Note** Change to dpns when sts no longer fit around circular needle.)
Work chart rnds 33–45—10 sts rem.
Cut yarn, leaving about a 12" tail, and thread into a yarn needle. Run through the open sts twice.

Finishing
Weave in ends. Block lightly. ■

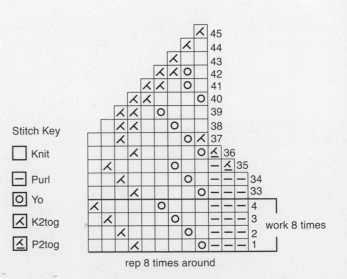

Stitch Key

- ☐ Knit
- ⊟ Purl
- ⊙ Yo
- ⊼ K2tog
- ⊿ P2tog

work 8 times

rep 8 times around

Three-Button Cardigan

Three-Button Cardigan

This swingy cardigan knit in a lacy ribbed pattern is the perfect cover-up for spring. The upbeat shades of *Silk Garden* are as pretty as a bouquet of flowers.

Designed by Edna Hart

Skill Level: ■■□□

Materials

- 8 (9, 11, 12, 13, 18) 1¾oz/50g skeins (each approx 110yd/100m) of Noro *Silk Garden* (silk/mohair/wool) in #302
- Size 7 (4.5mm) circular needle, 40"/100cm long, OR SIZE TO OBTAIN GAUGE
- Size E/4 (3.5mm) crochet hook
- Tapestry needle
- Three 1⅜"/34mm buttons

Sizes

Sized for X-Small (Small, Medium, Large, X-Large, XX-Large)

Knitted Measurements

Bust (closed) 30½ (36, 41, 46, 51, 56)"/77.5 (91.5, 104, 117, 129.5, 142)cm

Length 18½ (19½, 20½, 21½, 22½, 23½)"/47 (49.5, 52, 54.5, 57, 59.5)cm

Gauges

19 sts and 24 rows = 4"/10cm over puff ribbing.

22 sts and 30 rows = 4"/10cm over slip st ribbing.

TAKE TIME TO CHECK GAUGES.

Puff Ribbing

(multiple of 6 sts plus 5 more)

K3W K3, wrapping yarn twice around needle for each st.

Row 1 (RS) P4, *k3w, p3; rep from * to last st, p1.

Row 2 K4, *p3 (dropping extra loops), k3; rep from * to last st, k1.

Repeat rows 1 and 2 for pattern.

Slip Stitch Ribbing

(multiple of 6 sts plus 4 more)

Row 1 (RS) *P4, sl 2 wyib; rep from * to last 4 sts, p4.

Row 2 *K4, p2; rep from * to last 4 sts, k4.

Repeat rows 1 and 2 for pattern.

Back

Cast on 77 (89, 101, 113, 125, 137) sts.

Work 2 (2, 4, 4, 6, 6) rows in puff ribbing.

Dec row (RS) K1, ssk, work in pat to last 3 sts, k2tog, k1.

Work 2 (2, 4, 4, 4, 4) rows in pat as est.

Dec row (WS) P1, p2tog, work in pat to last 3 sts, p2tog tbl, p1.

Cont in pat as est, dec 1 st each side every 3rd row 5 times more, ending with a WS row—63 (75, 87, 99, 111, 123) sts.

Work 4 (4, 4, 6, 6, 6) rows even in pat.

Inc row (RS) K1, m1, work in pat to last st, m1, k1.

Cont in pat, work inc row every 8th row 4 times more—73 (85, 97, 109, 121, 133) sts.

Work even in pat until back measures 11½ (12, 12½, 13, 13½, 14)"/29 (30.5, 32, 33, 34, 35.5)cm from beg, ending with a WS row.

Armhole shaping

Bind off 3 (4, 5, 7, 9, 11) sts at beg of next 2 rows.

Dec row (RS) K1, ssk, work in pat to last 3 sts, k2tog, k1.

Rep dec row every RS row 2 (5, 6, 8, 10, 12) times more—

61 (65, 73, 77, 81, 85) sts. Work even in pat as est until armhole measures 5½ (6, 6½, 7, 7½, 8)"/14 (15, 16.5, 18, 19, 20.5)cm, ending with a WS row.

Neck and shoulder shaping

Work 23 (24, 27, 29, 30, 32) sts in pat, bind off next 15 (17, 19, 19, 21, 21) sts, work to end of row.

Right shoulder

Rows 1, 3 and 5 (WS) Work in pat to end of row.

Rows 2, 4 and 6 Bind off 2 sts, work in pat to end of row.

Rows 7 and 9 Bind off 5 (5, 6, 7, 7, 7) sts, work in pat to end of row.

Rows 8 and 10 Bind off 2 sts, work in pat to end of row.

Bind off rem 3 (4, 5, 5, 6, 8) sts.

Left shoulder

With WS facing, join yarn to left shoulder sts.

Rows 1, 3 and 5 (WS) Bind off 2 sts, work in pat to end of row.

Rows 2 and 4 Work in pat to end of row.

Rows 6 and 8 Bind off 5 (5, 6, 7, 7, 7) sts, work in pat to end of row.

Rows 7 and 9 Bind off 2 sts, work in pat to end of row.

Bind off rem 3 (4, 5, 5, 6, 8) sts.

Left Front

Cast on 35 (41, 47, 53, 59, 65) sts.

Work 2 (2, 4, 4, 6, 6) rows in puff ribbing.

Dec row (RS) K1, ssk, work in pat to end of row.

Work 2 (2, 4, 4, 4, 4) rows in pat.

Dec row (WS) Work in pat to last 3 sts, p2tog tbl, p1.

Cont in pat, dec every 3rd row 5 times more, ending with a WS row—28 (34, 40, 46, 52, 58) sts.

Work 4 (4, 4, 6, 6, 6) rows in pat as est.

Inc row (RS) K1, m1, work in pat to end of row.

Rep inc row every 8th row 4 times more—33 (39, 45, 51, 57, 63) sts.

Work even in pat until front measures 11½ (12, 12½, 13, 13½, 14)"/29 (30.5, 32, 33, 34, 35.5)cm from beg, ending with a WS row.

Armhole shaping

Row 1 (RS) Bind off 3 (4, 5, 7, 9, 11) sts, work in pat to end of row.

Row 2 Work in pat as est to end of row.

Dec row (RS) K1, ssk, work in pat to end of row.

Rep dec row every RS row 2 (5, 6, 8, 10, 12) times more—27 (29, 33, 35, 37, 39) sts.

Work even in pat until armhole measures 2 (2½, 3, 3½, 4, 4½)"/5 (6.5, 7.5, 9, 10, 11.5)cm, ending with a RS row.

Neck and shoulder shaping

Rows 1, 3 and 5 (WS) Bind off 2 sts, work in pat to end of row.

Rows 2, 4, 6, 8, 10, 12, 14, 16, 18, 20 and 22 Work in pat to end of row.

Rows 7, 9, 11, 13, 15, 17, 19, 21 and 23 P1, p2tog tbl, work in pat to end of row.

Work even until armhole measures 6½ (7, 7½, 8, 8½, 9)"/16.5 (18, 19, 20.5, 21.5, 23)cm.

Rows 24 and 26 Bind off 5 (5, 6, 7, 7, 7) sts, work in pat to end of row.

Rows 25 and 27 Rep row 2.

Bind off rem 2 (4, 6, 6, 8, 10) sts.

Right Front

Cast on 35 (41, 47, 53, 59, 65) sts.

Work 2 (2, 4, 4, 6, 6) rows in puff ribbing.

Dec row (RS) Work in pat to last 3 sts, k2tog, k1.

Work 2 (2, 4, 4, 4, 4) rows in pat.

Dec row (WS) P1, p2tog, work in pat to end of row.

Cont in pat, dec every 3rd row 5 times more, ending with a WS row—28 (34, 40, 46, 52, 58) sts.

Work 4 (4, 4, 6, 6, 6) rows in pat as est.

Inc row (RS) Work in pat to last st, m1, k1.

Rep inc row every 8th row 4 times more—33 (39, 45, 51, 57, 63) sts.

Work even in pat until front measures 11½ (12, 12½, 13, 13½, 14)"/29 (30.5, 32, 33, 34, 35.5)cm from beg, ending with a RS row.

Armhole shaping

Row 1 (WS) Bind off 3 (4, 5, 7, 9, 11) sts, work in pat to end of row.

Dec row (RS) Work in pat to last 3 sts, k2tog, k1.

Rep dec row every RS row 2 (5, 6, 8, 10, 12) times more—27 (29, 33, 35, 37, 39) sts.

Work even in pat until armhole measures 2 (2½, 3, 3½, 4, 4½)"/5 (6.5, 7.5, 9, 10, 11.5)cm ending with a WS row.

Neck and shoulder shaping

Rows 1, 3 and 5 (RS) Bind off 2 sts, work in pat to end of row.

Rows 2, 4, 6, 8, 10, 12, 14, 16, 18, 20 and 22 Work in pat to end of row.

Rows 7, 9, 11, 13, 15, 17, 19, 21 and 23 P1, p2tog tbl, work in pat to end of row.

Work even until armhole measures 6½ (7, 7¼, 8, 8¼, 9)"/16.5 (18, 19, 20.5, 21.5, 23)cm.

Rows 24 and 26 Bind off 5 (5, 6, 7, 7, 7) sts, work in pat to end of row.

Rows 25 and 27 Rep row 2.

Bind off rem 2 (4, 6, 6, 8, 10) sts.

Sleeves

Cast on 59 (65, 65, 71, 71, 71) sts.

Work 2 (2, 4, 4, 6, 6) rows in puff ribbing.

(*Continued on page 138.*)

Zigzag Scarf

Zigzag Scarf

This garter-stitch scarf zigs and zags through the subtle color changes of *Silk Garden* yarn.

Designed by Katharine Hunt

Skill Level: ■■□□

Materials

■ 4 1¾oz/50g balls (each approx 110yd/100m)
of Noro *Silk Garden* (silk/mohair/lamb's wool) in #323
■ One pair size 8 (5mm) knitting needles
OR SIZE TO OBTAIN GAUGE

Knitted Measurements

Approx 5¼" wide x 90" long

Gauge

19 sts and 32 rows = 4"/10cm over garter st using size 8 (5mm) needles. TAKE TIME TO CHECK GAUGE.

Notes

1) For ease of working, mark RS of work with a safety pin.
2) In garter stitch, each ridge counts as 2 rows.

Scarf

Lower triangle
Cast on 1 st.
Row 1 (WS) K1.
Row 2 K into front, back and front of st on needle—3 sts.
Row 3 Knit.
Row 4 Kfb, knit to last st, kfb—2 sts inc'd.
Rep rows 3 and 4 ten times more—25 sts.
Next row (WS) Knit.
*Zig
Row 1 (RS) Kfb, knit to last 2 sts, k2tog.
Row 2 Knit.
Rep rows 1 and 2 seven times more, completing 8 ridges.
Zag
Row 1 (RS) Ssk, knit to last st, kfb.
Row 2 Knit.
Rep rows 1 and 2 seven times more, completing 8 ridges.
Rep from * 20 times more.
Top triangle
Row 1 (RS) Ssk, knit to last 2 sts, k2tog—2 sts dec'd.
Row 2 Knit. Rep rows 1 and 2 ten times more—3 sts.
Next row (RS) Sl 1, k2tog, psso. Fasten off last st.

Finishing

Weave in ends. Block. ■

Cowl Neck Tunic

Cowl Neck Tunic

Deep earth tones and an assortment of cables create a warm and richly textured fabric. The tunic-length and cowl neck are fashion at its most up-to-date!

Designed by Michele Wang

Skill Level: ■■■□

Materials

- 9 (10, 12, 14, 15) 1¾oz/50g skeins (each approx 110yd/100m) of Noro *Kureyon* (wool) in #149
- Size 8 (5mm) circular needles, 16"/40cm and 24"/60cm long, OR SIZE TO OBTAIN GAUGE
- Size 9 (5mm) 16"/40cm circular needle
- Cable needle
- Tapestry needle

Sizes

Sized for Small (Medium, Large, X-Large, XX-Large)

Knitted Measurements

Bust 35½ (39, 44½, 49, 54)"/90 (99, 113, 125, 137)cm
Length 33½ (33¾, 36¼, 36¼, 38)"/85 (85.5, 92, 92.5, 96.5)cm

Gauges

16 sts and 26 rows = 4"/10cm over reverse St st using size 8 (5mm) needles.
14 sts and 24 rows of oval cable measures 2¾" W x 3¾" H/7cm x 9.5cm
TAKE TIME TO CHECK GAUGES.

Notes

1) Back is longer than front, creating a sort of tail-flap.
2) Tunic is vented on both sides.
3) Braided edge along bottom and armhole opening is knit separately and sewn on as part of the finishing.
4) Use a loose bind-off for the cowl neck stitches.

Stitch Glossary

RC Sl 1 st to cn and hold to *back*, k1, k1 from cn.
LC Sl 1 st to cn and hold to *front*, k1, k1 from cn.
4-st RC Sl 2 sts to cn and hold to *back*, k2, k2 from cn.
4-st LC Sl 2 sts to cn and hold to *front*, k2, k2 from cn.
3-st RPC Sl 1 st to cn and hold to *back*, k2, p1 from cn.
3-st LPC Sl 2 sts to cn and hold to *front*, p1, k2 from cn.
6-st RC Sl 3 sts to cn and hold to *back*, k3, k3 from cn.

Reverse Stockinette Stitch

Row 1 (RS) Purl.
Row 2 Knit.
Rep rows 1 and 2 for pat.

Braid

(over 4 sts)
Row 1 (RS) RC, LC.
Row 2 Purl.
Rep rows 1 and 2 for pat.

Right Cable

(over 4 sts)
Row 1 (RS) Knit.
Row 2 Purl.

Row 3 4-st RC.

Row 4 Purl.

Rep rows 1–4 for pat.

Left Cable

(over 4 sts)

Row 1 (RS) Knit.

Row 2 Purl.

Row 3 4-st LC.

Row 4 Purl.

Rep rows 1–4 for pat.

Oval Cable

(over 14 sts)

Set-up row 1 (RS) P4, k6, p4.

Set-up row 2 K4, p6, k4.

(**Note** These two set-up rows are only worked once at the beginning of the back and of the front.)

Rows 1 and 5 (RS) K4, 6-st RC, K4.

Rows 2, 4 and 6 K4, p6, k4.

Row 3 P4, k6, p4.

Row 7 P3, 3-st RPC, k2, 3-st LPC, p3.

Row 8 K3, [p2, k1] twice, p2, k3.

Row 9 P2, 3-st RPC, p1, k2, p1, 3-st LPC, p2.

Rows 10, 12, 14, 16, 18 and 20 [K2, p2] 3 times, k2.

Rows 11, 13, 15, 17 and 19 [P2, k2] 3 times, p2.

Row 22 K3, [p2, k1] twice, p2, k3.

Row 23 P2, 3-st LPC, p1, k2, p1, 3-st RPC, p2.

Row 24 Rep row 2. Rep rows 1–24 for pat.

Back

With size 8 (5mm) 24"/60cm circular needle, cast on 82 (88, 98, 106, 116) sts.

Row 1 (RS) K1, p to last st, k1.

Row 2 Knit.

Next row (RS) Work 4 sts of braid, work 8 (11, 16, 20, 25) sts in reverse St st, [work 4 sts of right cable, work 14 sts of oval cable] twice, work 4 sts of left cable, work 14 sts of oval cable, work 4 sts of left cable, work 8 (11, 16, 20, 25) sts in reverse St st, work 4 sts of braid.** Work even in pats as est until back measures 7"/18cm, ending on a WS row.

Next row (RS) Work 12 (15, 20, 24, 29) sts in reverse St st, [work 4 sts of right cable, work 14 sts of oval cable] twice, work 4 sts of

left cable, work 14 sts of oval cable, work 4 sts of left cable, work 12 (15, 20, 24, 29) sts in reverse St st. Work 7 rows in pats as est.

Dec row (RS) P2, p2tog, work in pat to last 4 sts, p2tog tbl, p2.

Rep dec row every 8th row 7 (7, 9, 9, 10) times more—66 (72, 78, 86, 94) sts. Work 6 rows even in pats as est.

Inc row (RS) P2, m1P, work in pat to last 2 sts, m1P, p2.

Rep inc row every 6th (6th, 4th, 4th, 4th) row 7 (7, 9, 9, 10) times more—82 (88, 98, 106, 116) sts.

Cont even in pats as est until back measures 25½ (25½, 27¾, 27¾, 29)"/65 (65, 70.5, 70.5, 73.5)cm from beg.

Armhole shaping

Bind off 4 (5, 6, 7, 8) sts at beg of next 2 rows.

Bind off 2 (3, 4, 5, 6) sts at beg of foll 2 rows.

Bind off 1 (1, 2, 2, 2) sts at beg of next 4 (4, 2, 4, 4) rows.

Bind off 0 (0, 1, 1, 1) sts at beg of next 0 (0, 4, 2, 6) rows—66 (68, 70, 72, 74) sts.

Cont even in pats as est until armhole measures 7 (7¼, 7½, 7¾, 8)"/18 (18.5, 19, 19.5, 20.5)cm, ending with a WS row.

Neck and shoulder shaping

Bind off 4 (4, 5, 5, 5) sts at beg of next 2 rows.

Next row (RS) Bind off 4 (4, 4, 4, 5) sts, work 16 sts in pat, bind off next 18 (20, 20, 22, 22) sts, work in pat to end.

Left shoulder

Bind off 4 (4, 4, 4, 5) sts at beg of next row, then bind off 4 sts at beg of next 3 rows. Bind off rem 4 sts.

Right shoulder

With WS facing, join yarn to shoulder sts.

Bind off 4 sts at beg of next 3 rows. Bind off rem 4 sts.

Front

Work as for back to **. Work even in pats as est until front measures 3"/7.5cm, ending on a WS row.

Continue same as for back until armhole measures 5 (5¼, 5½, 5¾, 6)"/12.5 (13.5, 14, 14.5, 15)cm, ending with a WS row.

Neck and shoulder shaping

Next row (RS) Work 27 (28, 29, 30, 31) sts in pat, bind off next 12 sts, work in pat to end.

Right neck and shoulder

Bind off 3 sts at beg of next RS row.

Bind off 2 sts at beg of foll 2 (3, 3, 3, 3) RS rows.

Bind off 1 (0, 0, 2, 2) sts at beg of next RS row.

Bind off 4 (4, 5, 5, 5) sts at beg of next WS row, bind off 1 st at beg of next RS row. (*Continued on page 139.*)

Leaf Lace Socks

Leaf Lace Socks

Kick up your heels in lacy little socks knit in vibrant shades of *Silk Garden Sock Yarn.*

Designed by Judy Sumner

Skill Level: ■■■□

Materials

■ 1 3½oz/100g ball (approx 330yd/300m)of Noro *Silk Garden Sock Yarn* (lamb's wool/silk/nylon/mohair) in #264

■ 1 set (5) double-pointed needles (dpns) size 2 (2.75mm) OR SIZE TO OBTAIN GAUGE

Knitted Measurements

Foot circumference 8"/20.5cm
Foot length (heel to toe) 10"/25.5cm
Length (heel to cuff) 10"/25.5cm

Gauges

24 sts and 32 rows = 4"/10cm over St st using size 2 (2.75mm) needles
26 sts and 32 rows = 4"/10cm over Leaf Chart (unstretched) using size 2 (2.75mm) needles
TAKE TIME TO CHECK GAUGES.

Twisted Rib

(over an even number of sts)
Rnd 1 *K1 tbl, p1; rep from * around.
Rep rnd 1 for twisted rib.

Sock

Cast on 48 sts and divide sts evenly over 4 dpns—12 sts per needle. Work in twisted rib for 1½"/3.8cm. Work rnds 1–24 of Leaf Chart twice. Sock measures approx 7½"/19cm from beg. With same needle just used (Needle 4), k12 from Needle 1—24 sts on one needle for heel flap. Work back and forth in rows over these sts as foll:

Heel Flap
(**Note** Sl sts purlwise with yarn at WS of work.)
Row 1 (WS) Sl 1, p23.
Row 2 (RS) [Sl 1, k1] 12 times.
Rep rows 1 and 2 eleven times more, then work row 1 once more.
Turn Heel
Row 1 (RS) Sl 1, k13, SKP, k1, turn.
Row 2 (WS) Sl 1, p5, p2tog, p1, turn.
Row 3 Sl 1, k6, SKP, k1, turn.
Row 4 Sl 1, p7, p2tog, p1, turn.
Row 5 Sl 1, k8, SKP, k1, turn.
Row 6 Sl 1, p9, p2tog, p1, turn.
Row 7 Sl 1, k10, SKP, k1, turn.
Row 8 Sl 1, p11, p2tog, p1, turn.
Row 9 Sl 1, k12, SKP, turn.
Row 10 Sl 1, p12, p2tog—14 sts. Turn.
Gussets
Next rnd With Needle 1, k across 14 heel sts, then pick up and k13 sts along side of heel flap, M1 in loop between heel flap and instep needle; with Needle 2, work in pat as established over first

instep needle; with Needle 3, work in pat over 2nd instep needle; with Needle 4, M1 in loop between instep needle and heel flap, pick up and k13 sts along side of heel flap, then k7 from Needle 1—21 sts each on Needles 1 and 4, 12 sts each on Needles 2 and 3.

Next rnd K to last 2 sts of Needle 1, k2tog, work in pat across instep sts, k2tog on Needle 4, k to end.

Dec rnd K to last 3 sts of Needle 1, SKP, k1, work instep sts as established, with Needle 4, k1, k2tog, k to end.

Next rnd Work even.

Rep last 2 rnds 7 times more—12 sts on each needle.

Foot

Work even through rnd 24 of Leaf Chart. Cont in St st over all sts until foot length is 1½" less than desired length from back of heel.

Toe

Dec rnd K to last 3 sts of Needle 1, SKP, k1; on Needle 2, k1, k2tog, k to end; k to last 3 sts of Needle 3, SKP, k1; on Needle 4, k1, k2tog, k to end.

Next rnd Knit.

Rep last 2 rnds until 5 sts rem on each needle.

K across first needle, move sts so that there are 10 sts on each of 2 needles and graft sts tog. ∎

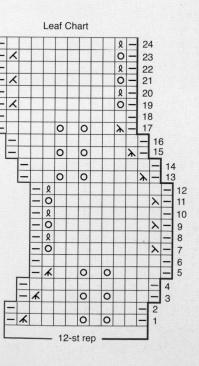

Stitch Key

☐	Knit
—	Purl
O	Yo
ℓ	K1 tbl
⋌	K2tog
⋋	Ssk
⋌	K3tog
⋋	SK2P

Leaf Chart

12-st rep

Trinity Stitch Sweater

Trinity Stitch Sweater

This chic, loose-fitting sweater is made up of individual strips that are joined as the piece is knit. No shaping required!

Designed by Valentina Devine

Skill Level: ■■■□

Materials

- 5 (5, 6, 7) 3½oz/100g balls (each approx 220yd/200m) of Noro *Taiyo* (cotton/silk/wool/nylon) in #1
- One pair size 10 (6mm) needles OR SIZE TO OBTAIN GAUGE
- Size D (3.25mm) crochet hook
- Four split st markers

Sizes

Sized for Small (Medium, Large, X-Large). Shown in size Small.

Knitted Measurements

Bust 40 (43, 48, 51)"/102 (109, 122, 130)cm
Length 18 (19, 20, 21)"/46 (48, 51, 53)cm
Upper arm 16 (17, 18, 19)"/41 (43, 46, 48)cm

Gauge

22 sts and 20 rows = 4"/10cm over trinity st using size 10 needles.
TAKE TIME TO CHECK GAUGE.

Trinity Stitch

(over a multiple of 4 sts, plus 2)
(**Note** Sl sts purlwise with yarn in front.)
Rows 1 and 3 (RS) K1 tbl, p to last st, sl 1.
Row 2 K1 tbl, *p3tog, [k1, p1, k1] into next st; rep from * to last st, sl 1.
Row 4 K1 tbl, *[k1, p1, k1] into next st, p3tog; rep from * to last st, sl 1.
Rep rows 1–4 for trinity st.

Note

If you want to change the color flow, break the strand and use alternately from the inside and the outside of the yarn ball.

Back

Strip 1

Cast on 22 (26, 22, 26) sts. Work in trinity st until strip measures 18 (19, 20, 21)"/46 (48, 51, 53) cm, end with a RS row. Bind off loosely on WS.

Strip 2

Cast on 22 sts. Work in trinity st and join to Strip 1 as foll:
Rows 1 and 3 (RS) K1 tbl, p to last st, sl 1, do not turn, insert LH needle from front to back under 2 strands at edge of Strip 1, sl last st from RH needle onto LH needle, p3tog.
Row 2 K1 (through front loop), *p3tog, [k1, p1, k1] into next st; rep from * to last st, sl 1.
Row 4 K1, *[k1, p1, k1] into next st, p3tog; rep from * to last st, sl 1.
Rep rows 1–4 until strip is same length as Strip 1 and each edge st of Strip 1 has been worked, end with a RS row. Bind off loosely on WS.

Strips 3–4 (3–4, 3–5, 3–5)

Work as for Strip 2.

Strip 5 (5, 6, 6)

Cast on 22 (26, 22, 26) sts. Work as for Strip 2.

Front

Work as for back.

Sew shoulder seams, leaving 8 (8, 9, 9)" open at center for neck opening.

Sleeves

With RS facing, count down 20 (21, 22, 24) edge sts from shoulder seam on front and back and place a marker on each side for armhole.

Strip 1

Cast on 22 sts. Work as for Strip 2 of body until sleeve fits between front and back markers, end with a RS row. Bind off loosely on WS.

Strip 2

Work as for Strip 2 of body.

Finishing

Sew side and sleeve seams. With RS facing and crochet hook, work 1 row sc around sleeve and neck opening edges.

Crocheted edging with drawstring

Row 1 With RS facing and crochet hook, beg at side seam and work 1 row sc around lower edge of body (a multiple of 3 sts, plus 2). Join with sl st to first st. Do not turn.

Row 2 Ch 3 (counts as first dc), *1 dc in next sc, ch 2, skip 1 sc, 1 dc in next sc; rep from *, end 1 dc in next sc, ch 2, skip 1 sc, join with sl st to top of ch.

Row 3 *1 sc, ch 3, sl st in 3rd chain from hook, 1 sc; rep from *. Fasten off last st.

Make a ch st drawstring as foll: work a chain 40" long, or desired length, then beg in 2nd ch from hook, work 1 sc in each ch to end. Fasten off. Tie a knot at each end of drawstring. Weave drawstring through ch-2 spaces in edging. ∎

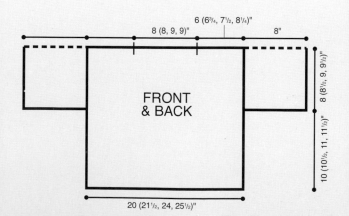

Modular Afghan

Modular Afghan

Hexagon-shaped motifs are joined as they are knit to create a kaleidoscope of swirling colors.

Designed by Anna-Beth Meyer-Graham

Skill Level: ■■■□

Materials
- 6 3½oz/100g balls (each approx 220 yd/200m) of Noro *Taiyo* (cotton/silk/wool/nylon) in #15
- One set (4) size 8 (5mm) double-pointed needles (dpns) OR SIZE TO OBTAIN GAUGE
- One set (5) size 8 (5mm) double-pointed needles (dpns)
- Yarn needle

Knitted Measurements
Approx 45" x 40"/114.5cm x 101.5cm

Gauge
One hexagon motif measures approx 5" x 6"/12.5cm x 15cm.
TAKE TIME TO CHECK GAUGE.

Notes
1) Each hexagon is knit from the outside in. Rather than making them individually and sewing them tog, you work each new hexagon by picking up sts at edges of previous hexagons and casting on rem sts.
2) For the maximum number of color combinations when using a slowly variegating yarn such as *Taiyo*, try rewinding about half your skeins so the color variegates in the opposite direction.
3) Use knit-on cast-on throughout.

Afghan
Hexagon 1
Cast on 60 sts and divide evenly over 3 dpns—20 sts per needle. Join, being careful not to twist. Work rnds 1–15 of Hexagon Chart—6 sts. Cut yarn, leaving a tail, and use a yarn needle to go through the rem sts twice, pull the yarn snug. Go through sts twice more. Weave in ends.

Hexagon 2
On first hexagon, 6 defined ridges radiate out from the center to the edges. Referring to Joining Diagram 1, pick up a st right where one of those ridges meets the edge by inserting RH needle from back to front in an edge st, then working from right to left, pick up 9 more sts along the edge, ending just before tip of next ridge. Attach yarn and cast on 10 more sts onto same needle, then 20 sts each on 2 more needles—60 sts. Work as for Hexagon 1.

Hexagon 3
With RS facing and referring to Joining Diagram 2, pick up 10 sts between 2 ridges on Hexagon 1, then pick up 10 more sts along edge of Hexagon 2. Cast on another 40 sts onto 2 more needles—60 sts. Work as for Hexagon 1.

Hexagons 4–61
Cont to add hexagons as established, foll Joining Diagram 3 for placement.

Finishing
Block to measurements. ■

Stitch Key

☐ Knit
⊟ Purl
⊡ Yo
⊠ K2tog
⊠ K3tog

Hexagon Chart

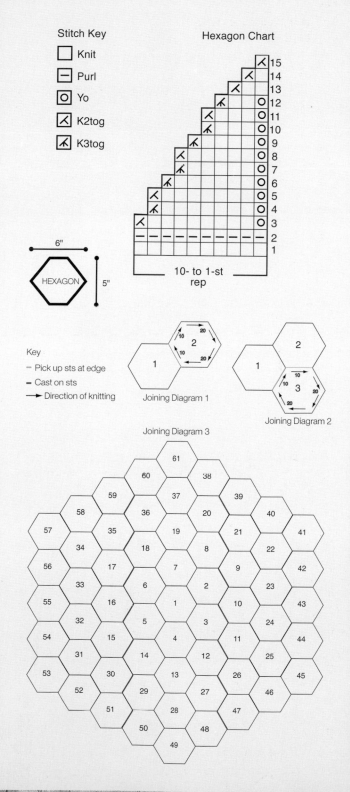

10- to 1-st rep

6"

HEXAGON 5"

Key

– Pick up sts at edge
▬ Cast on sts
→ Direction of knitting

Joining Diagram 1

Joining Diagram 2

Joining Diagram 3

Bobble Wrap

Bobble Wrap

Playful bobbles dance across a field of seed stitch and stockinette stitch stripes in this festive shawl.

Designed by Terri Johnson

Skill Level: ■■■□

Materials

- 4 1¾oz/50g balls (each approx 110 yd/100m) of Noro Yarns *Kureyon* (wool) in #170
- Size 8 (5mm) circular needle, 36"/91cm long, OR SIZE TO OBTAIN GAUGE

Knitted Measurements

Width across top 60"/152.5cm
Length at center back 21"/53.5cm

Gauge

15 sts and 22 rows = 4"/10cm over seed st using size 8 (5mm) needles. TAKE TIME TO CHECK GAUGE.

Stitch Glossary

Make Bobble (MB) [Knit into front, back, front, back, front] of next st—5 sts. Turn, p5. Turn, k5. Turn, p5. Turn, k3tog, k2tog, sl first st over 2nd st—1 st rems.

Seed Stitch

(over an odd number of sts)
Row 1 *P1, k1; rep from *, end p1.
Row 2 K the purl sts and p the knit sts.
Rep row 2 for seed st.

Wrap

Cast on 3 sts.
Row 1 (WS) Kfb, k1, kfb—5 sts.
Row 2 (RS) Kfb, p1, k1, p1, kfb—7 sts.
Row 3 Kfb, *k1, p1; rep from * to last 2 sts, k1, kfb—9 sts.
Row 4 Kfb, *p1, k1; rep from * to last 2 sts, p1, kfb—11 sts.
Rows 5–12 Rep rows 3 and 4 four times—27 sts.
Row 13 Rep row 3—29 sts.
Row 14 Kfb, [p1, k1] 6 times, p1, MB, [p1, k1] 6 times, p1, kfb—31 sts.
Row 15 Kfb, [k1, p1] 6 times, k1, p3, [k1, p1] 6 times, k1, kfb—33 sts.
Row 16 Kfb, [p1, k1] 6 times, p1, k5, [p1, k1] 6 times, p1, kfb—35 sts.
Row 17 Kfb, [k1, p1] 6 times, k1, p7, [k1, p1] 6 times, k1, kfb—37 sts.
Row 18 Kfb, [p1, k1] 6 times, p1, k9, [p1, k1] 6 times, p1, kfb—39 sts.
Row 19 Kfb, [k1, p1] 6 times, k1, p11, [k1, p1] 6 times, k1, kfb—41 sts.
Row 20 Kfb, [p1, k1] 6 times, p1, MB, k to last 15 sts, MB, [p1, k1] 6 times, p1, kfb—43 sts.
Rows 21 and 23 Kfb, [k1, p1] 6 times, k1, p to last 14 sts, [k1, p1] 6 times, k1, kfb.
Rows 22 and 24 Kfb, [p1, k1] 6 times, p1, k to last 14 sts, [p1, k1] 6 times, p1, kfb.
Row 25 Rep row 21—53 sts.
Rows 26–37 Rep rows 20–25 twice more—77 sts.
Row 38 Kfb, [p1, k1] 6 times, p1, [MB, k23] twice, MB, [p1, k1] 6 times, p1, kfb—79 sts.

Row 39 Kfb, [k1, p1] 6 times, k1, p24, k1, p1, k1, p24, [k1, p1] 6 times, k1, kfb—81 sts.

Row 40 Kfb, [p1, k1] 6 times, p1, k24, [p1, k1] twice, p1, k24, [p1, k1] 6 times, p1, kfb—83 sts.

Row 41 Kfb, [k1, p1] 6 times, k1, p24, [k1, p1] 3 times, k1, p24, [k1, p1] 6 times, k1, kfb—85 sts.

Row 42 Kfb, [p1, k1] 6 times, p1, k24, [p1, k1] 4 times, p1, k24, [p1, k1] 6 times, p1, kfb—87 sts.

Row 43 Kfb, [k1, p1] 6 times, k1, p24, [k1, p1] 5 times, k1, p24, [k1, p1] 6 times, k1, kfb—89 sts.

Row 44 Kfb, [p1, k1] 6 times, p1, MB, k23, MB, work row 2 of seed st to last 39 sts, MB, k23, MB, [p1, k1] 6 times, p1, kfb—91 sts.

Rows 45 and 47 Kfb, [k1, p1] 6 times, k1, p24, work seed st to last 38 sts, p24, [k1, p1] 6 times, k1, kfb.

Rows 46 and 48 Kfb, [p1, k1] 6 times, p1, k24, work seed st to last 38 sts, k24, [p1, k1] 6 times, p1, kfb.

Row 49 Rep row 45—101 sts.

Rows 50–109 Rep rows 44-49 ten times more—221 sts.

Rows 110 and 111 Rep rows 44 and 45 once—225 sts.

Row 112 Kfb, [p1, k1] 7 times, M1 purl, *k1, p1; rep from * to last 16 sts, k1, M1 purl, [p1, k1] 7 times, kfb—229 sts.

Row 113 Kfb, *k1, p1; rep from * to last 2 sts, k1, kfb—231 sts.

Row 114 Kfb, *p1, k1; rep from * to last 2 sts, p1, kfb—233 sts. Bind off all sts in pat. ■

Modular Vest

Modular Vest

This graphic vest is as fun to knit as it is to wear. The modular construction showcases the shades of *Taiyo* brilliantly.

Designed by Linda Cyr

Skill Level: ■■■□

Materials

- 3 (4, 5) 3½oz/100g balls (each approx 220 yd/200m) of Noro *Taiyo* (cotton/silk/wool/nylon) in #3
- Size 7 (4.5mm) needles OR SIZE TO OBTAIN GAUGE
- Stitch holders or 2 size 7 (4.5mm) dpns to be used as holders
- Size I/9 (5.5mm) crochet hook

Sizes

Sized for Small (Medium, Large)

Finished Measurements

Bust 36 (40, 44)"/91.5 (101.5, 111.5)cm
Length 24½ (26, 27½)"/62 (66, 70)cm

Gauge

17 sts and 34 rows = 4"/10cm over garter st. TAKE TIME TO CHECK GAUGE.

Note

Always slip the first stitch of each row purlwise with yarn in back.

Vest Half (make 2)

Section 1
Cast on 32 (34, 36) sts.
Row 1 (RS) Sl 1, k to end.
Row 2 Sl 1, k to last 2 sts, k2tog.
Rep rows 1 and 2 until 16 (17, 18) sts rem.
Next row (RS) Sl 1, k to end.
Place sts on holder.

Section 2
With RS facing, rotate piece to work along the ends of rows. Pick up and k15 (16, 17) sts evenly across the left side of Section 1.
Rows 1–31 (33, 35) Sl 1, k to end.
Place sts on holder.

Section 3
With WS facing, rotate piece to work across side of just finished section and place held sts of previous section onto a needle. Pick up and k15 (16, 17) sts evenly across side of just finished section; k14 (15, 16), k2tog from needle—30 (32, 34) sts. Work same as Section 1, starting with row 1.

Section 4
With RS facing, rotate piece to work along ends of rows of just finished section and place held sts of previous section onto a needle. Pick up and k15 (16, 17) sts evenly across side of just finished section; k13 (14, 15), k2tog from needle—29 (31, 33) sts. Work same as Section 1, starting with row 1.

Section 5
Work as for Section 3.

Section 6
Work as for Section 4.

Section 7
Work as for Section 3.

Section 8
Work as for Section 4 until last row.

Last row Bind off all sts, leaving last loop on needle.

Section 9
Work as for Section 3.

Section 10
Work as for Section 2.

Sections 11–16
Work as for Sections 3–8.

Section 17
Work as for Section 3 except cont in pat until 2 sts rem.
Bind off.

Side Panels (make 2)
Make a slip knot and place on needle.

Row 1 (RS) K1, yo, k1.

Row 2 Sl 1, m1, k to end.

Rep row 2 until there are 18 (24, 30) sts, ending with a WS row.

Next row Sl, m1, k to last 2 sts, k2tog.

Next row Sl 1, k to end.

Rep last 2 rows until side of piece measures 7 (7½, 8)"/18 (19, 20.5)cm, ending with a WS row.

Dec row Sl 1, k to last 2 sts, k2tog.

Rep dec row until 2 sts rem.
Bind off.

Ties (make 4)
Cast on 6 sts.

Row 1 Sl 1, k to end.

Rep row 1 until piece measures 8"/20.5cm.
Bind off.

Finishing
Lightly steam block all pieces.

(**Note** Seams can be sewn together or slip-stitched together with a crochet hook.)

Place vest halves with shorter edges together and sew back seam. Fold fronts over back at shoulders and position side panels 8 (8½, 9)"/20.5 (21.5, 23)cm down from shoulders. Sew to fronts and back. Position ties as desired and sew to fronts. ■

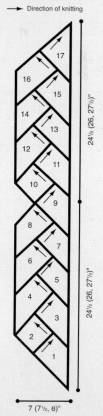

→ Direction of knitting

17
16
15
14
13
12
11
10
9
8
7
6
5
4
3
2
1

24½ (26, 27½)"

24½ (26, 27½)"

SIDE PANEL

7 (7½, 8)"

4 (5, 6)"

7 (7½, 8)"

Lacy Gaiter

Kimono Cardigan

Kimono Cardigan

This easy-fitting cardigan with three-quarter-length sleeves and a single-button closure proves that comfort and style are not mutually exclusive.

Designed by Debbie O'Neill

Skill Level: ■■☐☐

Materials

- 8 (9, 11, 12, 13, 14) 1¾oz/50g skeins (each approx 110yd/100m) of Noro *Silk Garden* (silk/mohair/wool) in #279
- Size 7 (4.5mm) needles OR SIZE TO OBTAIN GAUGE. (**Note** It is useful to have one extra needle in the size used for knitting the sweater.)
- Stitch holders
- One 1"/2.5cm (or larger) button
- Tapestry needle

Sizes

Sized for X-Small (Small, Medium, Large, X-Large, XX-Large)

Finished Measurements

Bust 34 (38, 41, 44, 46, 50)"/86.5 (96.5, 104, 111.5, 117, 127)cm
Length 22¼ (23¼, 24¼, 25¼, 26¼, 27¼)"/56.5 (59, 61.5, 64, 66.5, 69)cm

Gauges

18 sts and 24 rows = 4"/10cm in St st.
18 sts and 32 rows = 4"/10cm in garter st.
TAKE TIME TO CHECK GAUGES.

Note

This sweater is designed to have an oversized fit with 4"/10cm of wearing ease.

Back

Cast on 53 (55, 57, 60, 62, 64) sts. Work in garter st until back measures 17 (19, 20½, 22, 23, 25)"/43 (48, 52, 56, 58.5, 63.5)cm. Bind off all sts loosely, leaving last st on needle. Rotate piece to work across the long edge.
Pick up and k75 (85, 91, 99, 103, 111) sts evenly across—76 (86, 92, 98, 104, 112) sts.
Work 6 rows in garter st, beg with a WS row.
Work in St st, beg with a WS row, until piece measures 10½ (11, 11½, 12, 12½, 13)"/26.5 (28, 29, 30.5, 31.5, 33)cm from pick-up edge.
Next row (RS) K24 (29, 31, 34, 36, 40), bind off next 28 (28, 30, 30, 32, 32) sts, k to end of row—24 (29, 31, 34, 36, 40) sts each shoulder. Place sts on holders.

Right Front

Cast on 53 (55, 57, 60, 62, 64) sts. Work in garter st until front measures 9 (10, 10¾, 11½, 12, 13)"/23 (25.5, 27.5, 29, 30.5, 33)cm. Bind off all sts loosely, leaving last st on needle. Rotate piece to work across the short edge.
Pick up and k40 (45, 48, 51, 54, 58) sts evenly across—41 (46, 49, 52, 55, 59) sts.
Work 6 rows in garter st, beg with a WS row.
Next row (WS) P to last 5 sts, k5.
Next row Knit.
Cont in St st, keeping 5 edge sts in garter st, for 1½"/4cm, ending with a WS row.
Divide for buttonhole
Next row (RS) K3, join a second ball of yarn, k to end of row.

Cont in St st with garter st edge over the two sets of stitches for ½"/1.5cm to form a vertical buttonhole. Then work in pat to end of row using single ball of yarn to end buttonhole.

Neck shaping

Dec row (RS) K5, ssk, k to end of row.

Rep dec row every RS row 11 (11, 12, 12, 13, 13) times more—29 (34, 36, 39, 41, 45) sts.

Cont in pat as est until front measures same as back. Place 24 (29, 31, 34, 36, 40) shoulder sts on holder, and garter st edge sts on another holder.

Left Front

Cast on 53 (55, 57, 60, 62, 64) sts. Work in garter st until front measures 9 (10, 10¾, 11½, 12, 13)"/23 (25.5, 27.5, 28, 30.5, 33)cm. Bind off all sts loosely, leaving last st on needle. Rotate piece to work across the short edge.

Pick up and k40 (45, 48, 51, 54, 58) sts evenly across—41 (46, 49, 52, 55, 59) sts.

Work 6 rows in garter st, beg with a WS row.

Next row (WS) K5, p to end of row.

Next row Knit.

Cont in St st, keeping 5 edge sts in garter st, for 2"/5cm, ending with a WS row.

Neck shaping

Dec row (RS) K to last 7 sts, k2tog, k5.

Rep dec row every RS row 11 (11, 12, 12, 13, 13) times more—29 (34, 36, 39, 41, 45) sts.

Cont in pat as est until front measures same as back. Place 24 (29, 31, 34, 36, 40) shoulder sts on holder, and garter st edge sts on another holder.

Sleeves

Cast on 70 (74, 78, 84, 88, 92) sts. Work 6 rows of garter st, then work in St st until sleeve measures 9½ (10, 10¼, 10½, 10½, 11¼)"/24 (25.5, 26, 26.5, 26.5, 28.5)cm or desired length from beg. Bind off all sts loosely.

Finishing

Join shoulder using 3-needle bind-off. Center sleeves at shoulder seams and set into armholes. Sew sleeve seams from cuff to armhole. Sew side seams from hem to armhole.

Neckband

With RS facing, using a spare needle, pick up and k28 (28, 30, 31, 32, 32) sts across back neck; k across garter st edge sts from left front.

Row 1 (WS) K4, k last st of garter st edge together with next st of back neck.

Row 2 K5.

Rep rows 1 and 2 until all back neck sts have been worked. Join rem 5 sts to garter st edge of right front using 3-needle bind-off. Weave in all ends. Block to measurements. Sew button opposite buttonhole. ■

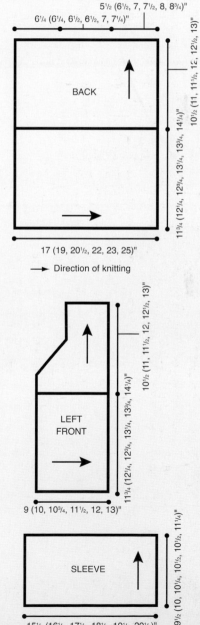

5½ (6½, 7, 7½, 8, 8¾)"

6¼ (6¼, 6½, 6½, 7, 7¼)"

BACK

10½ (11, 11½, 12, 12½, 13)"

11¾ (12¼, 12¾, 13¼, 13¾, 14¼)"

17 (19, 20½, 22, 23, 25)"

→ Direction of knitting

10½ (11, 11½, 12, 12½, 13)"

LEFT FRONT

11¾ (12¼, 12¾, 13¼, 13¾, 14¼)"

9 (10, 10¾, 11½, 12, 13)"

SLEEVE

9½ (10, 10¼, 10½, 10½, 11¼)"

15½ (16½, 17½, 18½, 19½, 20½)"

Sideways Stripes Vest

Sideways Stripes Vest

This clever design starts with a provisional cast-on in the back and is worked sideways to the front, creating a vertical striped pattern.

Designed by Cheryl Murray

Skill Level: ■■□□

Materials

- 4 (4, 4, 5, 5, 6) 3½oz/100g skeins (each approx 220 yd/200m) of Noro *Taiyo* (cotton/silk/wool/nylon) in #13
- Size 8 (5mm) 32" circular needle, 32"/80cm long, OR SIZE TO OBTAIN GAUGE
- Size 8 (5mm) double-pointed needles (dpns)
- Smooth waste yarn
- Size H/5mm crochet hook
- Three 1"/25mm decorative buttons (LaMode #23311)
- Two ¾"/19mm flat buttons (Slimline #Z307)

Sizes
Sized for X-Small (Small, Medium, Large, X-Large, XX-Large)

Knitted Measurements
Bust (closed) 32 (35, 38, 40, 44, 47)"/81 (89, 96.5, 101.5, 111.5, 119.5)cm
Length 17¾ (18½, 19½, 20½, 21¼, 22¼)"/45 (47, 49.5, 52, 54, 56.5)cm

Gauge
18 sts and 36 rows = 4"/10cm in garter stripe pattern
TAKE TIME TO CHECK GAUGE.

Garter Stripe Pattern
Rows 1–23 Knit.
Row 24 (WS) Purl.
Repeat rows 1–24 for pattern.

Left Back/Front
With waste yarn, cast on 80 (84, 88, 92, 96, 100) sts using crochet cast-on method. K 1 row. Turn and mark to indicate RS.
Back neck
Work 24 (24, 26, 26, 30, 30) rows of garter stripe pat.
Inc row (RS) K1, m1, k to end.
Working 23 (23, 21, 21, 41, 41) more rows in garter stripe pat, rep inc row every RS row twice more—83 (87, 91, 95, 99, 103) sts.
Cont in garter st for 5 (6, 8, 10, 1, 2) ridges more, ending with a WS row.
Armhole shaping
Next row (RS) Bind off 31 (34, 36, 38, 38, 40) sts, k to end—52 (53, 55, 57, 61, 63) sts.
K 1 row.
Dec row (RS) K1, ssk, k to end.
Cont in garter st, work dec row every RS row 3 times more—48 (49, 51, 53, 57, 59) sts.
Work even in garter st until there are 10 (13, 16, 19, 12, 14) ridges from last St st stripe, ending with a RS row.
P 1 WS row.
Cont in garter st until there are 2 (4, 10, 12, 14, 18) ridges, ending with a WS row.
Inc row (RS) K1, m1, k to end.
Cont in garter st, work inc row every RS row 3 times more—52 (53, 55, 57, 61, 63) sts.
Cast on 31 (34, 36, 38, 38, 40) sts at beg of next RS row—83 (87, 91, 95, 99, 103) sts.
Cont in garter st until there are 10 (13, 16, 19, 12, 14) ridges from last St st stripe, ending with a RS row.
P 1 WS row.

Work 20 (20, 18, 18, 38, 38) rows of garter stripe pat, ending with a WS row.

Neck Shaping
Bind off 4 sts at beg of next RS row, bind off 3 sts at beg of foll RS row—76 (80, 84, 88, 92, 96) sts.

P 1 WS row.

Cont in garter stripe pat, bind off 2 sts at beg of next 24 (25, 26, 27, 28, 29) RS rows—28 (30, 32, 34, 36, 38) sts. AT THE SAME TIME, when 30 (32, 34, 36, 38, 40) sts rem, work interior buttonholes on WS row as folls: K2, yo, k2tog, work to last 4 sts, k2tog, yo, k2. Bind off all sts.

Right Back/Front
Back neck
With RS facing, pick up 80 (84, 88, 92, 96, 100) sts from crochet cast-on. P 1 WS row.

Work 24 (24, 26, 26, 30, 30) rows of garter stripe pat.

Inc row (RS) K to last st, m1, k1.

Working 23 (23, 21, 21, 41, 41) more rows in garter stripe pat, rep inc row every RS row twice more—83 (87, 91, 95, 99, 103) sts.

Cont in garter st for 5 (6, 8, 10, 1, 2) ridges, ending with a RS row.

Armhole shaping
Next row (WS) Bind off 31 (34, 36, 38, 38, 40) sts, k to end—52 (53, 55, 57, 61, 63) sts.

Dec row (RS) K to last 3 sts, k2tog, k1.

Cont in garter st, work dec row every RS row 3 times more—48 (49, 51, 53, 57, 59) sts.

Work even in garter st until there are 10 (13, 16, 19, 12, 14) ridges from last St st stripe, ending with a RS row.

P 1 WS row.

Cont in garter st until there are 2 (4, 10, 12, 14, 18) ridges, ending with a WS row.

Inc row (RS) K to last st, m1, k1.

Cont in garter st, work inc row every RS row 3 times more—52 (53, 55, 57, 61, 63) sts.

Cast on 31 (34, 36, 38, 38, 40) sts at beg of next WS row—83 (87, 91, 95, 99, 103) sts.

Cont in garter st until there are 10 (13, 16, 19, 12, 14) ridges from last St st stripe, ending with a RS row.

P 1 WS row.

Work 20 (20, 18, 18, 38, 38) rows of garter stripe pat, ending with a RS row.

Neck shaping
Bind off 4 sts at beg of next WS row, bind off 3 sts at beg of foll WS row—76 (80, 84, 88, 92, 96) sts.

P 1 WS row. Cont in garter stripe pat, bind off 2 sts at beg of next 24 (25, 26, 27, 28, 29) WS rows—28 (30, 32, 34, 36, 38) sts. Bind off.

Finishing
Sew shoulder seams.

Armhole edging (attached I-cord)
With circular needle, start at the center of underarm and pick up and k 60 (64, 68, 72, 72, 76) sts evenly around armhole. Cut yarn. With dpn, cast on 3 sts. *K2, ssk last st together with one st from armhole edge, DO NOT TURN, slide sts to other end of dpn; rep from * until all armhole sts have been bound off. Sew ends. Repeat for other armhole.

Front edging (attached I-cord)
With circular needle, starting at lower rght front edge, pick up and k 28 (30, 32, 34, 36, 38) sts along right front, 56 (58, 60, 62, 64, 66) sts along right neck edge, 36 (36, 38, 38, 42, 42) sts along back neck, 56 (58, 60, 62, 64, 66) sts along left neck edge, 28 (30, 32, 34, 36, 38) sts along left front edge—204 (212, 222, 230, 242, 250) sts. Cut yarn. With dpn, cast on 3 sts. Work attached I-cord as above until 6 (6, 6, 6, 7, 7) body sts have been attached, then work 4"/10cm of unattached I-cord (K3, slide) for button loop, [work attached I-cord until 8 (9, 10, 11, 11, 12) sts have been attached, work 4"/10cm of unattached I-cord] twice, work attached I-cord until 6 (6, 6, 6, 7, 7) body sts have been attached.

Corners
Work 1 st in unattached I-cord on either side of each corner st to create a sharp, neat corner.

Cont in attached I-cord around all rem sts, working left front corner st as above. Bind off.

Using a small amount of yarn from a contrasting section of the color sequence, tightly wrap the bases of all buttonhole loops and secure yarn. Attach decorative buttons to left front opposite the buttonhole loops.

Carefully sew backing buttons to the inside of right front opposite interior buttonholes. Avoid allowing sewing thread to show on vest front. ■

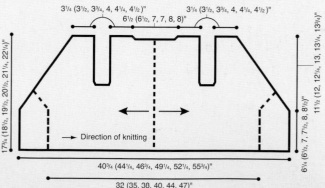

Parasol Lace Vest

Parasol Lace Vest

Acidic shades of *Taiyo* give this vest
an edge, and the striped, ribbed waistband
balances the lace front panels.

Designed by Edna Hart

Skill Level: ■■■□

Materials

- 3 (4, 4, 5) 3½oz/100g skeins (each approx 220 yd/
200m) of Noro *Taiyo* (cotton/silk/wool/nylon) in #8
- Size 8 (5mm) circular needle, 40"/100cm long,
OR SIZE TO OBTAIN GAUGE
- One ¾"/2cm button

Sizes

Sized for Small (Medium, Large, X-Large)

Knitted Measurements

Bust (closed) 36 (39, 44, 46.5)"/91.5 (99, 112, 118)cm
Length 22½ (23, 23½, 24)"/57 (58.5, 59.5, 61)cm

Gauges

18 sts and 24 rows = 4"/10cm over faux pleat pat.
16 sts and 26 rows = 4"/10cm over parasol st.
TAKE TIME TO CHECK GAUGES.

Faux Pleat Pattern

(multiple of 7 sts plus 5 more)
Row 1 (RS) *K5, p2; rep from * to last 5 sts, k5.
Row 2 P5, *k2, p5; rep from * to end.
Rep rows 1 and 2 for faux pleat pat.

Parasol Stitch

(over 21 sts)
Row 1 (RS) K2, yo, k1, [p3, k1] 4 times, yo, k2.
Row 2 and all WS rows Purl.
Row 3 K3, yo, k1, [p3, k1] 4 times, yo, k3.
Row 5 K4, yo, k1, [p3, k1] 4 times, yo, k4.
Row 7 K5, yo, k1, [p2tog, p1, k1] 4 times, yo, k5.
Row 9 K6, yo k1, [p2tog, k1] 4 times, yo, k6.
Row 11 K7, yo, k1, [k3tog, k1] twice, yo, k7.
Row 12 Purl.
Rep rows 1–12 for parasol st.

Vest

Upper back

Cast on 70 (77, 91, 98) sts.
Row 1 (RS) K1 (selvage st), work in faux pleat pat to last st, k1
(selvage st). Work 5 rows in faux pleat pat, maintaining selvage
sts in St st throughout.
Inc row (RS) K1, m1, work in pat to last st, m1, k1.
Cont in pat as est, work inc row every 6th (6th, 6th, 8th, 10th) row
5 (5, 3, 2) times more and incorporating increased stitches into
faux pleat pat—82 (89, 99, 104) sts.
Work even in pat as est until back measures 8 (7½, 7, 6½)"/20.5
(19, 18, 16.5)cm, ending with a WS row.
Armhole shaping
Bind off 6 (8, 12, 14) sts at beg of next 2 rows—70 (73, 75, 76) sts.

Work even in pat as est until armhole measures 7½ (8, 8½, 9)"/19 (20.5, 21.5, 23)cm, ending with a WS row.

Neck and shoulder shaping

Bind off 7 sts at beg of next 2 rows.

Next row (RS) Work 12 sts in pat, join a 2nd ball of yarn and bind off next 32 (35, 37, 38) sts, work in pat to end.

Working both sides at once, bind off 6 sts at shoulder edge each side twice.

Upper right front lace panel

Cast on 7 sts, p 1 row; cast on 7 sts, k 1 row; cast on 7 sts, p 1 row—21 sts.

Work in parasol stitch until panel measures 16"/40.5cm, ending with row 11.

Rows 12 and 14 (WS) Bind off 7 sts, p to end.

Rows 13 and 15 Knit.

Bind off rem 7 sts.

Upper left front lace panel

Cast on 7 sts, k 1 row; cast on 7 sts, p 1 row; cast on 7 sts—21 sts.

Work 8 repeats of parasol stitch, ending with row 12.

Rows 13 and 15 (RS) Bind off 7 sts, k to end.

Rows 14 and 16 Purl.

Bind off rem 7 sts.

Upper right side panel

Cast on 10 (13, 16, 20) sts. Work 2 rows in St st.

Shaping row (RS) K1, k2tog, k to last st, m1, k1.

Rep shaping row every 6th row 5 times more. Work even in St st until panel measures 8 (7½, 7, 6½)"/20.5 (19, 18, 16.5)cm. Bind off.

Sew dec edge of panel to lace panel.

Upper left side panel

Cast on 10 (13, 16, 20) sts. Work 2 rows in St st.

Shaping row (RS) K1, m1, k to last 3 sts, ssk, k1.

Rep shaping row every 6th row 5 times more. Work even in St st until panel measures 8 (7½, 7, 6½)"/20.5 (19, 18, 16.5)cm. Bind off.

Sew dec edge of panel to lace panel.

Sew shoulder seams and side seams.

Lower rib

With RS facing, pick up and k130 (143, 163, 178) sts evenly across lower edge of vest, matching faux pleat sts across the back.

Row 1 (WS) K3 (0, 0, 0), p5 (4, 0, 4), k2 (2, 2, 2), *p5, k2; rep from * to last 8 (4, 0, 4) sts, p5 (4, 0, 4), k3 (0, 0, 0).

Work 3 rows in faux pleat pat as est, placing markers after stitches 30 (33, 36, 40) and 100 (110, 120, 131) to indicate side seams.

Inc row (RS) [Work in faux pleat pat to 1 st before marker, kfb, slip marker, kfb], work in pat to end.

Cont in pat as est, work inc row every 6th row 5 (6, 5, 6) times more and incorporating increased stitches into faux pleat pat—154 (171, 187, 202) sts. Work even in pat as est until lower rib measures 6½ (7, 7½, 8)"/16.5 (18, 19, 20.5)cm from pick-up. Bind off.

Armbands

With RS facing, starting at underarm seam, pick up and k78 (88, 98, 108) sts evenly around armhole. K 6 rows. Bind off and sew seam. Repeat for other armhole.

Front and neck band

With RS facing, starting at lower right front, pick up and k234 (239, 244, 251) sts evenly around front opening. K 3 rows.

Buttonhole row (RS) K to 2 sts before lower rib seam, k2tog, ssk, k to end.

Next row K to center of decreased sts of previous row, cast on 2 sts, k to end.

K 1 row. Bind off.

Finishing

Block garment to measurements. Sew on button opposite buttonhole. Weave in ends. ■

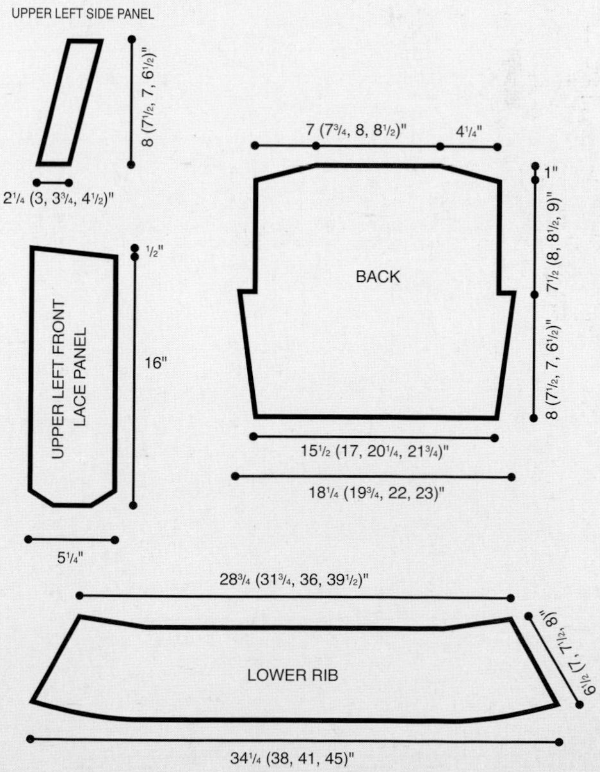

UPPER LEFT SIDE PANEL
8 (7½, 7, 6½)"
2¼ (3, 3¾, 4½)"
UPPER LEFT FRONT LACE PANEL
½"
16"
5¼"
7 (7¾, 8, 8½)"
4¼"
1"
BACK
7½ (8, 8½, 9)"
8 (7½, 7, 6½)"
15½ (17, 20¼, 21¾)"
18¼ (19¾, 22, 23)"
28¾ (31¾, 36, 39½)"
LOWER RIB
6½ (7, 7½, 8)"
34¼ (38, 41, 45)"

Block Cardigan

Block Cardigan

This boxy cardigan is knit in components that are joined and edged in basic black, making the colors of *Silk Garden* pop.

Designed by Peggy Forester

Skill Level: ■■□□

Materials

- 2 1¾oz/50g skeins (each approx 109 yd/98m) of Noro *Silk Garden* (silk/mohair/wool) in #323 (A)
- 2 (2, 2, 3, 3, 3) balls in #293 (B)
- 2 (2, 2, 3, 3, 3) balls in #302 (C) and #272 (D)
- 3 (4, 4, 5, 5, 6) balls in #308 (E)
- 1 ball in #301 (F)
- 3 1⅖oz/40g skeins (each approx 99yd/89m) of Noro *Cash Iroha* (silk/wool/cashmere/nylon) in #02 (G)
- Size 8 (5mm) needles OR SIZE TO OBTAIN GAUGE
- Size 6 (4.25mm) needles
- Size 6 (4.25mm) double-pointed needles (dpn)
- Four 1" (2.5cm) square buttons

Sizes

Sized for X-Small (Small, Medium, Large, X-Large, XX-Large)

Knitted Measurements

Bust 34 (38, 42, 46, 50, 54)"/86.5 (96.5, 106.5, 117, 127, 137)cm
Length 23 (23½, 24, 24½, 25, 25½)"/58.5 (59.5, 61, 62, 63.5, 64.5)cm

Gauge

18 sts and 26 rows = 4"/10cm over St st using size 8 (5mm) needles
TAKE TIME TO CHECK GAUGE.

Sleeves

With larger needles and G, cast on 54 (56, 60, 62, 64, 66) sts.
K 6 rows. Change to A.
Inc row (RS) K2, m1, k to last 2 sts, m1, k2.
Cont in St st, work inc row every 14th (14th, 16th, 14th, 10th, 10th) row 3 (2, 6, 7, 4, 4) times more, then every 16th (16th, 0, 0, 12th, 12th) row 3 (4, 0, 0, 5, 5) times—68 (70, 74, 78, 84, 86) sts.
AT THE SAME TIME, when sleeve measures 7 (7¼, 7½, 7¾, 7¾, 7¾)"/18 (18.5, 19, 19.5, 19.5., 19.5)cm from beg, change to G and k 6 rows.
Change to B and complete shaping, cont in St st until sleeve measures 16 (16½, 17, 17¼, 17¼, 17¼)"/40.5 (42, 43, 45, 45, 45)cm from beg. Change to G and k 6 rows. Bind off.

Upper Back

(**Note** This section is worked side to side.)
With larger needles and C, cast on 43 (45, 45, 45, 49, 49)sts.
Work in St st for 8 (9, 10, 11, 12, 13)"/20.5 (23, 25.5, 28, 30.5, 33)cm.
Change to G and k 6 rows.
Change to D and work in St st for 8 (9, 10, 11, 12, 13)"/20.5 (23, 25.5, 28, 30.5, 33)cm.
Bind off loosely.

Upper Left Front

With larger needles and D, cast on 35 (39, 44, 48, 53, 57) sts.
Beg with a k row, work in St st until front measures 7½ (8, 8, 8, 9, 9)"/19 (20.5, 20.5, 20.5, 23, 23)cm, end with a RS row.
Neck shaping
Row 1 (WS) Bind off 7 (8, 8, 9, 9, 9) sts, p to end of row.
Rows 2, 4 and 6 Knit.
Rows 3, 5 and 7 Bind off 2 sts, p to end of row—22 (25, 30, 33, 38, 42) sts.
Work even in St st until front measures 9½ (10, 10, 10, 11, 11)"/24 (25.5, 25.5, 25.5, 28, 28)cm from beg.
Bind off loosely.

Upper Right Front

With larger needles and D, cast on 35 (39, 44, 48, 53, 57) sts. Beg with a p row, work in St st until front measures 7½ (8, 8, 8, 9, 9)"/19 (20.5, 20.5, 20.5, 23, 23)cm, end with a WS row.

Neck shaping

Row 1 (RS) Bind off 7 (8, 8, 9, 9, 9) sts, k to end of row.

Rows 2, 4 and 6 Purl.

Rows 3, 5 and 7 Bind off 2 sts, k to end of row—22 (25, 30, 33, 38, 42) sts. Work even in St st until front measures 9¼ (10, 10, 10, 11, 11)"/24 (25.5, 25.5, 25.5, 28, 28)cm from beg. Bind off loosely.

Lower Back

With larger needles and E, cast on 76 (84, 95, 102, 112, 120) sts. K 3 rows. Work even in St st until back measures 12½ (12½, 13, 14, 14, 15)"/31.5 (31.5, 33, 35.5, 35.5, 38)cm from beg. Bind off.

Lower Fronts (make 2)

With larger needles and E, cast on 35 (39, 44, 48, 53, 57) sts. K 3 rows. Work even in St st until front measures 12½ (12½, 13, 14, 14, 15)"/31.5 (31.5, 33, 35.5, 35.5, 38)cm from beg. Bind off.

Finishing

Steam lightly and block pieces to measurements. Sew shoulder seams. Center and set in sleeves. Sew lower fronts and back to upper fronts and back. Sew sleeve and side seams.

Buttonband

With smaller needles and G, pick up and k114 (118, 120, 126, 128, 134) sts along left front edge. Work 10 rows in k1, p1 rib. Bind off in pat.

Buttonhole band

With smaller needles and G, pick up and k114 (118, 120, 126, 128, 134) sts along right front edge. Work 4 rows in k1, p1 rib.

Buttonhole row (WS) Work 10 sts in rib, bind off 3 sts, *work 15 sts in rib, bind off 3 sts; rep from * twice more, work in rib to end of row.

Next row Work in rib, casting on 3 sts over each bound-off space. Work 4 rows more in rib. Bind off in pat.

Neckband

With smaller needles and G, pick up and k95 (99, 99, 103, 103, 103) sts evenly around neck edge, including front bands. Work 5 rows in rib beg with p1.

Buttonhole row (RS) Work 3 sts in rib, bind off 3 sts, work in rib to end of row.

Next row Work in rib, casting on 3 sts over bound-off space. Work 3 rows more in rib. Bind off in pat.

I-cord edging

With dpn and F, cast on 4 sts. *Slide sts to other end of needle, k4; rep from * until cord is long enough to go around neck, fronts and entire lower edge slightly stretched. Bind off. Sew I-cord onto edges of cardigan as pictured. Sew buttons opposite buttonholes. ∎

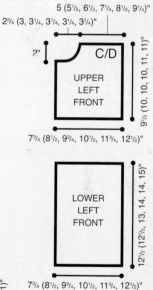

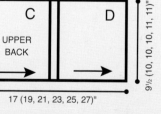

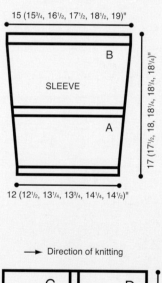

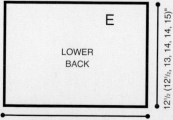

Rainbow Knee-Highs

Rainbow Knee-Highs

These ruffle-edged knee-high socks are so fun and colorful you won't want to hide them under shoes or boots.

Designed by Barb Brown

Skill Level: ■■■■

Materials

- 3 3½oz/100g balls (each approx 330 yd/300m) of Noro *Silk Garden Sock Yarn* (lamb's wool/silk/nylon/mohair) in #87
- One set (4) size 2 (2.75mm) double-pointed needles (dpn), OR SIZE TO OBTAIN GAUGE
- One size 3 (3.25mm) circular needle, 16"/40cm long
- Stitch markers

Knitted Measurements

Foot circumference 8"/20.5cm
Calf circumference (unstretched) 10"/25.5cm
Foot length (heel to toe) 9½"/24cm

Gauge

28 sts and 40 rows = 4"/10cm over St st using size 2 (2.75mm) needles. TAKE TIME TO CHECK GAUGE.

Knee-Highs

With circular needle, cast on 243 sts. Place marker (pm) and join, being careful not to twist sts. Knit 1 rnd.

Beg eyelet rib

Rnds 1 and 2 *P3, k6; rep from * around.

Rnd 3 *P3, k2tog, k2, ssk; rep from * around—189 sts.

Rnd 4 *P3, k4; rep from * around.

Rnd 5 *P3, k2tog, ssk; rep from * around—135 sts.

Rnd 6 *P3, k2; rep from * around.

Rnd 7 *P2, SK2P; rep from * around—81 sts.

Rnd 8 *P3, cast on 6 sts, using backward-loop method; rep from * around—243 sts.

Rep rnds 1–8 once more, then work rnds 1–7 once—81 sts.

Body

Change to dpns (27 sts on each needle). K 1 rnd. P 1 rnd.

Turn work inside out (for cuff turn-back) and work as foll:

Rnds 1–17 *K2, p1; rep from * around.

Rnd 18 [K2, p1] 4 times, pm, [k2, p1] 18 times, k2, pm, p1, [k2, p1] 4 times.

Beg calf shaping panel

Rnds 1–4 Work rib as established to marker, sl marker (sm), k to marker, sm, work rib as established to end of rnd.

Rnd 5 (dec rnd) Work rib as established to 3 sts before marker, k2tog, p1, sm, k to marker, sm, p1, ssk, work rib as established to end.

Rep rnds 1–5 nine times more—61 sts (5 sts rem in shaping panel).

Next rnd K1, p1, k to last 3 sts of rnd, sm (this is new beg-of-rnd marker), place last 3 sts on Needle 1 and cont as foll, removing other 2 markers when you come to them:

Next 3 rnds [P1, k1] twice, p1, k to end.

Dec rnd P1, S2KP, p1, k to end—59 sts.

Next 4 rnds P1, k1, p1, k to end.

Dec rnd S2KP, k to end—57 sts.

Next 4 rnds P1, k to end.

Dec rnd K2tog, k to end—56 sts.

Work in St st until piece measures 13"/33cm (or desired length) from cuff turn-back row, ending last rnd 14 sts before end of rnd.

Place next 28 sts on one needle for heel flap. Place rem 28 sts on 2 needles to hold for instep.

Heel flap

(**Note** Sl sts purlwise with yarn at WS of work.)

Row 1 (RS) *S1, k1; rep from * to end.

Row 2 Sl 1, p to end. [Rep rows 1 and 2] 14 times more.

Turn heel

Row 1 (RS) K15, ssk, k1, turn.

Row 2 (WS) S1, p3, p2tog, p1, turn.

Row 3 Sl 1, k4, ssk, k1, turn.

Row 4 Sl 1, p5, p2tog, p1, turn.

Row 5 Sl 1, k6, ssk, k1, turn.

Row 6 Sl 1, p7, p2tog, p1, turn.

Row 7 Sl 1, k8, ssk, k1, turn.

Row 8 Sl 1, p9, p2tog, p1, turn.

Row 9 Sl 1, k10, ssk, k1, turn.

Row 10 Sl 1, p11, p2tog, p1, turn.

Row 11 Sl 1, k12, ssk, k1, turn.

Row 12 Sl 1, p13, p2tog, p1, turn—16 sts.

Row 13 K16, do not turn.

Gusset

With RS facing and Needle 1, pick up and k16 sts along side of heel flap; with Needle 2, k28 instep sts; with Needle 3, pick up and k16 sts along other side of heel flap, then k8 heel sts, ending in middle of heel. Sl rem 8 sts of heel onto end of Needle 1—24 sts each on Needles 1 and 3, 28 sts on Needle 2 (for instep).

Rnd 1 K to 9 sts before instep, [k1, p1] 4 times, k1, k across instep sts, [k1, p1] 4 times, k1, k to end of rnd.

Rnd 2 K to 9 sts before instep, work rib as established to 2 sts before instep, k2tog, k across instep sts, ssk, work in pat as established to end of rnd.

Rnd 3 Work in pat as established to 1 st before instep, k1, k across instep sts, k1, work in pat as established to end of rnd.

Rep rnds 2 and 3 until there are 56 sts—14 sts each on Needles 1 and 3 and 28 sts on Needle 2. Work even in St st until foot measures 2½"/6.5cm less than total desired length.

Shape toe

Rnd 1 Needle 1: k to last 3 sts, k2tog, k1; Needle 2: k1, ssk, k to last 3 sts, k2tog, k1; Needle 3: k1, ssk, k to end.

Rnd 2 Knit.

Rep rnds 1 and 2 six times more—28 sts. Rep rnd 1 only twice more—20 sts. Place sts of Needles 1 and 3 onto one needle—10 sts on each of 2 needles. Graft sts tog. Weave in ends. Turn back cuff. ∎

Ruffled Wristers

Ruffled Wristers

Keep your hands warm (and colorful) in these playful fingerless mitts. Beginning with larger needles creates the ruffled effect.

Designed by Katharine Hunt

Skill Level: ■■■□

Materials

- 1 3½oz/100g balls (each approx 330 yd/300m) of Noro *Silk Garden Sock Yarn* (lamb's wool/silk/nylon/mohair) in #304
- One pair each sizes 4 and 6 (3.5mm and 4mm) needles OR SIZE TO OBTAIN GAUGE
- Four size 4 (3.5mm) double-pointed needles (dpn)
- 2 stitch markers
- 2 (3) small stitch holders (*safety pins are ideal*)
- Tapestry needle

Sizes

Sized for Small/Medium (Medium/Large); shown in size Small/Medium

Knitted Measurements

Circumference 7¼ (8½)"/18.5 (21.5)cm
Length 6 (7)"/15 (18)cm

Gauge

24 sts and 34 rows = 4"/10cm over St st, using smaller needles.
TAKE TIME TO CHECK GAUGE.

Wrister

With larger needles, cast on 85 (101) sts. Purl 1 row, knit 1 row, purl 1 row. Change to smaller needles. Knit 1 row.
Dec row (RS) Ssk, *p1, SK2P; rep from * to last 3 sts, p1, k2tog—43 (51) sts.
Next row (WS) *P1, k1; rep from *, end p1. Cont in rib pat as established until piece measures 2 (2½)"/5 (6.5)cm from beg, end with a WS row. Work in St st as foll: Work 4 rows even, ending with a WS row.

Thumb gusset

Row 1 (RS) K21 (25), place marker (pm), M1, k1, M1, pm, k21 (25)—45 (53) sts; 3 sts between markers.
Row 2 and all WS rows Purl.
Row 3 (inc row) K to marker, sl marker (sm), M1, k to marker, M1, sm, k to end—47 (55) sts; 5 sts between markers.
Rep inc row every other row 2 (4) times more, then every 4th row 2 (1) times—55 (65) sts; 13 (15) sts between markers.
Row 17 (RS) K to marker; sl 13 (15) gusset sts to holders, removing markers, cast on 5 (7) sts, k to end—47 (57) sts.
Row 19 K21 (25), ssk, k1 (3), k2tog, k to end—45 (55) sts.
Size M/L only: Row 21 K25, ssk, k1, k2tog, k to end—53 sts.
Both sizes: Row 21 (23) K21 (25), SK2P, k to end—43 (51) sts.
Work 5 (7) rows even. Work in k1, p1 rib for 3 rows. Bind off loosely in rib.

Thumb

With RS facing and 3 dpns, sl 13 (15) gusset sts from holders and pick up 5 (7) sts along cast-on edge—18 (22) sts. Join yarn and work as foll:
Rnd 1 Ssk, k9 (11), k2tog, k5 (7)—16 (20) sts.
Work in k1, p1 rib for 3 rnds. Bind off loosely in rib.

Finishing

Block gently, taking care not to stretch ribbing. Sew side seams. ■

Patchwork Afghan

Patchwork Afghan

Mitered squares knit in striking shades of *Taiyo* form the focal points of the dozens of blocks that are joined to create this dramatic afghan.

Designed by Dorcas Lavery

Skill Level: ■■■□

Materials

- 11 3½oz/100g balls (each approx 220yd/200m) of Noro *Taiyo* (cotton/silk/wool/nylon) in #7
- One pair size 8 (5mm) needles, OR SIZE TO OBTAIN GAUGE
- One pair size 8 (5mm) circular needle, 36"/91cm long
- Stitch marker
- Yarn needle

Knitted Measurements

Approx 42" x 56"/106.5cm x 142cm

Gauge

18 sts and 30 rows = 4"/10 over garter stitch, using size 8 (5mm) needles.
TAKE TIME TO CHECK GAUGE.

Notes

1) For ease of working, mark RS of work.
2) When picking up sts along edge, pick up in the "valley" between garter ridges.
3) Sl sts purlwise with yarn at WS of work.
4) To wrap a st, sl 1 wyib, bring yarn to front of work between needles, sl st back to LH needle.

Block (make 48)

Cast on 20 sts, using the long-tail method.
Row 1 (RS) Sl 1, k19.
Rows 2–18 Rep row 1.
Row 19 Sl 1, k9, wrap next st (see Note 4) and turn work.
Row 20 (WS) K10.
Rows 21–58 Sl 1, k9.
Row 59 (RS) Bind off 9 sts (1 st rems on RH needle), then pick up and k20 more sts evenly along left edge of piece, k rem 10 sts on LH needle—31 sts.
Row 60 Sl 1, k9, place marker, p1, k to end.
Row 61 Sl 1, k to 2 sts before marker, sl 2 as if to k2tog, remove marker, k1, p2sso, replace marker, k to end.
Row 62 Sl 1, k to marker, p1, k to end.
Rows 63–78 Rep rows 61 and 62 eight times more—13 sts.
Row 79 Rep row 61, but don't replace marker and do not turn at end of row, with RS still facing, pick up and k19 sts along edge of block—30 sts.
Rows 80–96 Sl 1, k29. Bind off all sts knitwise.

Finishing

Block pieces.
Assembly
Sew blocks tog in groups of 4, with the cast-on tails meeting in the middle (Diagrams 1 and 2).
Arrange these 4-block squares into 3 x 4 rows (Diagram 3) and join.
Border
With RS facing and circular needle, pick up and k174 sts along

one short side of afghan (29 sts per block). Knit 2 rows. Bind off all sts. Rep on other short side.

With RS facing and circular needle, pick up and k236 sts along one long side (29 sts per block, plus 2 sts along each border). Knit 2 rows. Bind off all sts. Rep on other long side.

Weave in all loose ends. ∎

Diagram 1

cast-on tail

Diagram 2

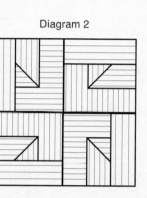

Diagram 3

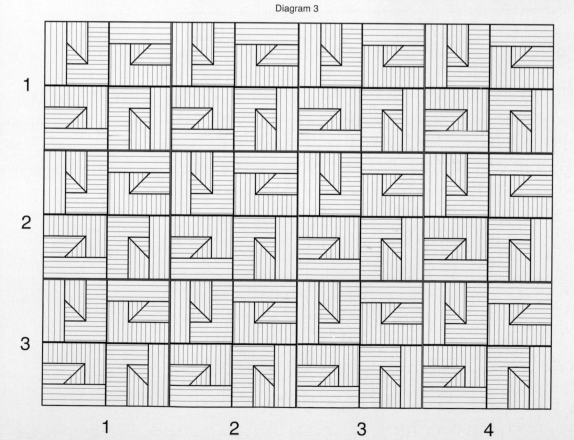

Felted Cloche

Felted Cloche

This colorful cap is knit in a single colorway of *Kureyon*, but alternating two balls of yarn creates dazzling stripes.

Designed by Tina Whitmore

Skill Level: ■■■□

Materials
- 2 1¾oz/50g balls (each approx 110 yd/100m) of Noro Yarns *Kureyon* (wool) in #270
- One size 10 (6mm) circular needle, 16"/40cm long, OR SIZE TO OBTAIN GAUGE
- Stitch marker
- Tapestry needle

Knitted Measurements (after felting)
Circumference 24"/61cm
Length 7¼"/18.5cm

Gauge (after felting)
16 sts and 36 rnds = 4"/10cm over pat st, using size 10 (6mm) needle. TAKE TIME TO CHECK GAUGE.

Pattern Stitch
Rnds 1–3 With A, knit.
Rnd 4 With B, knit.
Rnd 5 With B, purl.
Rep rnds 1–5 for pat.

Notes
1) Hat is worked circularly and finished before being felted.
2) Use two balls of yarn throughout, using one ball as A and the other as B. Start each ball of yarn at a different point in the color sequence, making sure there is sufficient contrast between A and B.
3) Carry yarn not being used loosely at the back of the work.

Hat
With A, cast on 96 sts. Place marker and join, being careful not to twist sts. Work rnds 1–5 of pat st 15 times, then work rnds 1–3 once more. Bind off.
Break yarns, leaving a long tail of A for finishing.

Finishing
*Sew first 3" and foll 3" of top of hat tog; rep from * 3 times more. You should have something resembling a plus sign at the top seam edge. Fold each corner down to the left and tack seamed edge only to body of hat (do not tack along fold edge).
Felt hat in washing machine or by hand. If felting by hand, place hat in hot soapy water and knead as you might a loaf of bread. You will feel a change in the texture of the yarn as it begins to felt. This may take about 10 minutes of kneading. Hat will begin to shrink as the fibers condense and become felted. Check hat often with measuring tape for size. You can halt the felting process immediately by rinsing the hat in cold water. Once desired size is reached, rinse out hat well in cool water and gently squeeze out excess moisture. Place hat on a bowl or form of similar size and mold into shape. Allow to air dry. Hat may take several days to become fully dry. ■

Striped Shawl

Striped Shawl

The alternating shades of *Kureyon* in this triangular wrap creates stripe patterns that are colorful yet subtle and sophisticated.

Designed by Tanis Gray

Skill Level: ■■■□

Materials
- 3 1¾oz/50g balls (each approx 110 yd/100m) of Noro Yarns *Kureyon* (wool) in #188 (A) and #252 (B)
- Size 8 (5mm) circular needle, 47"/119cm long, OR SIZE TO OBTAIN GAUGE
- Tapestry needle

Knitted Measurements
60"/152.5cm wide x 32"/81cm long

Gauge
13 sts and 23 rows = 4"/10cm over St st using size 8 (5mm) needle.
TAKE TIME TO CHECK GAUGE.

Stripe Pat
Work 8 rows with A, then 8 rows with B; rep from * for stripe pat.

Shawl
With A, cast on 251 sts. Work in stripe pat as foll:
Row 1 (RS) With A, k2, ssk, k120, S2KP, k120, k2tog, k2—247 sts.
Row 2 and all WS rows K2, p to last 2 sts, k2.
Row 3 K2, ssk, k118, S2KP, k118, k2tog, k2—243 sts.
Row 5 K2, ssk, k116, S2KP, k116, k2tog, k2—239 sts.
Row 7 K2, ssk, k114, S2KP, k114, k2tog, k2—235 sts.
Row 9 With B, k2, ssk, k112, S2KP, k112, k2tog, k2—231 sts.
Row 11 K2, ssk, k110, S2KP, k110, k2tog, k2—227 sts.
Row 13 K2, ssk, k108, S2KP, k108, k2tog, k2—223 sts.
Row 15 K2, ssk, k106, S2KP, k106, k2tog, k2—219 sts.
Cont in pat as established, working 2 fewer k sts on each side of center S2KP every RS row, until last row worked is:
Row 121 With B, k2, ssk, S2KP, k2tog, k2—7 sts.
Row 123 K2, S2KP, k2—5 sts.
Break yarn, weave through rem sts and secure on WS.

Finishing
Weave in all loose ends with tapestry needle. Block well. ∎

Fair Isle Cap

Fair Isle Cap

Knit with two constrasting colorways, this cap is fun to knit and showcases the wonderful color changes of *Kureyon*.

Designed by Carol Sulcoski

Skill Level: ■■■□

Materials

- 2 1¾oz/50g balls (each approx 110yd/100m) of Noro *Kureyon* (wool) in #242 (MC) and #95 (CC1 and CC2; see Notes)
- One size 8 (5mm) circular needle, 16"/40cm long, OR SIZE TO OBTAIN GAUGE
- Stitch holders
- One set size 8 (5mm) double-pointed needles (dpns)
- Stitch marker and holders

Knitted Measurements

Circumference 20¾"/53cm
Length 7¾"/20cm

Gauge

17 sts and 24 rnds = 4"/10cm over Fair Isle chart using size 8 (5mm) needle. TAKE TIME TO CHECK GAUGE.

Notes

1) Use one end of CC skein as CC1 and the other end of the skein as CC2.
2) As you work, if you do not like the color that is appearing or feel that it does not contrast enough with the other colors, break the yarn and rejoin it at another point in the color sequence.
3) Mark RS of each earflap with a safety pin.

Earflaps (make 2)

With CC1, cast on 1 st.
Row 1 (RS) K into front, back, front of st—3 sts.
Row 2 (WS) Knit.
Row 3 Kfb, k to last st, kfb—5 sts.
Rep rows 2 and 3 four times more—13 sts.
K 9 rows. Cut yarn. Place sts on a holder.

Hat

With circular needle and MC, cast on 88 sts. Place marker and join as foll: *place one earflap with RS facing you in front of sts on LH needle and [k 1 st of earflap tog with 1 cast-on st] 13 times*, k31, rep from * to * once, k rem 31 sts.
[P 1 rnd, k 1 rnd] 3 times, p 1 rnd.
Work 30 rnds of Fair Isle Chart.

Shape crown

(**Note** Change to dpns when sts no longer fit around circular needle.)
Rnd 1 With CC1, *k2, k2tog; rep from * around—66 sts.
Rnds 2 and 3 With CC2, knit.
Rnd 4 With CC2, *k1, k2tog; rep from * around—44 sts.
Rnd 5 With CC1, knit, dec 2 sts evenly around—42 sts.
Rnd 6 *K1 with CC2, k1 with CC1, k1 with CC2; rep from * around.
Rnd 7 With MC, knit.
Rnd 8 With MC, *k2tog; rep from * around—21 sts.
Rnd 9 *K2tog; rep from * to last st, k1—11 sts.
Rnd 10 Rep rnd 9—6 sts.
Break yarn and pull through rem sts.

Finishing

Weave in ends. Block.

I-cord ties (make 2)

With dpn and CC1, cast on 4 sts. Work I-cord for 14"/35.5cm. Bind off. Sew one cord to end of each earflap. ■

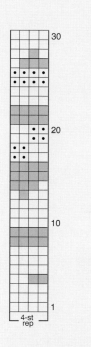

Color Key

- MC
- CC1
- CC2

Chevron Scarf

Chevron Scarf

Two shades of *Kureyon* combine to create shimmering stripes in this extra-long scarf.

Designed by Cheryl Kubat

Skill Level: ■■□□

Materials

- 3 1¾oz/50g balls (each approx 110 yd/100m) of Noro *Kureyon* (wool) in #259 (A) and #260 (B)
- One pair size 10 (6mm) knitting needles

OR SIZE TO OBTAIN GAUGE

Knitted Measurements

Approx 7½" x 90" after felting

Gauge (unfelted)

20 sts and 20 rows = 4"/10cm over chevron pat using size 10 (6mm) needles. TAKE TIME TO CHECK GAUGE.

Scarf

With A, cast on 45 sts.
Beg chevron pat
Row 1 (RS) K1, [kfb, k4, ssk, k2tog, k4, kfb] 3 times, k2.
Row 2 (WS) Purl.
Rows 3 and 4 With B, rep rows 1 and 2.
Rep rows 1–4 until desired length or until approx 10 yds of color A rem after having completed row 2.
Bind off loosely.

Finishing

Weave in ends. Lightly block edges, let dry. Then lightly felt by hand or washing machine. Lay flat to dry. ■

Hooded Vest

Hooded Vest

With a cozy hood, this tunic-length vest in autumnal browns and a cable and rib pattern is the perfect garment to see you through fall's chill.

Designed by Pat Olski

Skill Level: ■■■□

Materials

- 12 (15) 1¾oz/50g balls (each approx 110yd/100m) of Noro *Kureyon* (wool) in #242b
- Size 6 (4mm) needles OR SIZE TO OBTAIN GAUGE
- Spare needle (for 3-needle bind-off)
- Stitch markers
- Cable needles
- Stitch holders
- Optional closure (zipper, hook and eye or toggles)

Sizes

Sized for X-Small/Small (Medium/Large)

Knitted Measurements

Bust 37 (42¼)"/94 (107.5)cm
Length 27 (30)"/68.5 (76)cm

Gauges

15 sts and 24 rows = 4"/10cm over St st (blocked)
18 sts and 24 rows = 4"/10cm over cable pattern (blocked)
TAKE TIME TO CHECK GAUGES.

Stitch Glossary

8-st RC Sl 4 sts to cn and hold to *back*, k4, k4 from cn.
8-st LC Sl 4 sts to cn and hold to *front*, k4, k4 from cn.
6-st RPC Sl 2 sts to cn and hold to *back*, k4, p2 from cn.
6-st LPC Sl 4 sts to cn and hold to *front*, p2, k4 from cn.
TY Twist yarns around each other to avoid a hole at the join.

Long Cable and Rib Pattern

(multiple of 25 sts plus 5 more)
Set-up row 1 (RS) *K5, p6, k8, p6; rep from * to last 5 sts, k5.
Set-up row 2 P5, *k6, p8, k6, p5; rep from * to end.
Rows 1 and 9 *K2, yo, k2tog, k1, p6, 8-st LC, p6; rep from * to last 5 sts, k2, yo, k2tog, k1.
Row 2 and all WS rows Work each st as it appears; k the knit sts and p the purl sts and YOs.
Rows 3, 5 and 7 (RS) *K5, p6, k8, p6; rep from * to last 5 sts, k5.
Row 11 *K5, p4, 6-st RPC, 6-st LPC, p4; rep from * to last 5 sts, k5.
Rows 13, 15, 17, 19, 21, 23, 25 and 27 K5, p4, [k4, p4] twice; rep from * to last 5 sts, k5.
Row 29 *K5, p4, 6-st LPC, 6-st RPC, p4; rep from * to last 5 sts, k5.
Row 30 Rep row 2.
Rep rows 1–30 for pattern.

Note

In order to maintain striping sequence, select balls of yarn that appear to begin with the same color. The fronts are worked with 1 ball of yarn at a time. The back is worked with 2 similar balls of yarn, alternating every 2 rows so that the stripes appear to be similar in width to the 2 fronts. The hood is worked with 2 similarly colored balls, one for each side as for intarsia. Yarn from one ball is worked to the center, then twisted over the (TY) second ball to prevent a hole at the join.

Back

Cast on 91 (101) sts. Work in seed st for 11 rows.

Set-up row (RS) [K1, p1] twice, k2tog, p0 (5), work 80 sts in long cable and rib pat, p0 (5), pm for seed st edge, [k1, p1] twice, k1—90 (100) sts.

Set-up row 2 [K1, p1] twice, k1 (6), work 80 sts in long cable and rib pat, k1 (6), [k1, p1] twice.

Work in pat as est until back measures 15 (17)"/38 (43)cm from beg, ending with a WS row.

Side shaping

Dec row (RS) [K1, p1] twice, k1, ssk (p2tog tbl), work in pat to last 7 sts, k2tog (p2tog), [k1, p1] twice, k1.

Rep dec row every 6th row twice more—84 (94) sts.

Work even in pat as est until back measures 18 (20)"/46 (51)cm, ending with a WS row.

Armhole shaping

Next row (RS) Bind off 4 (5) sts (one k st on needle), [p1, k1] twice, p1, pm for seed st edge, work in pat to end.

Next row Bind off 4 (5) sts (one k st on needle), [p1, k1] twice, p1, pm for seed st edge, work in pat to end—76 (84) sts.

Work even in pats as est until armhole measures 8 (9)"/20.5 (23)cm, ending with a WS row.

Neck and shoulder shaping

Next row (RS) Work 25 (28) sts in pat, bind off next 26 (28) sts, work in pat to end.

Left shoulder

Next row (WS) Work in pat to last 3 sts, p2tog, p1.

Short row set 1 K1, k2tog, work 15 (18) sts in pat, w&t; work in pat to last 3 sts, p2tog, p1.

Short row set 2 K1, k2tog, work 12 (16) sts in pat, w&t; work in pat to end.

Place sts on holder.

Right shoulder

With WS facing, join yarn at neck edge.

Short row set 1 P1, p2tog tbl, work 15 (18) sts in pat, w&t; work in pat to last 3 sts, k2tog, k1.

Short row set 2 P1, p2tog tbl, work 12 (16) sts in pat, w&t; work in pat to last 3 sts, k2tog, k1.

Next row Work in pat to end. Place sts on holder.

Pockets (make 2)

Cast on 24 sts.

Row 1 (RS) K2, p4, k4, p4, k4, p4, k2.

Row 2 P2, k4, p4, k4, p4, k4, p2.

Rep rows 1 and 2 until piece measures 9½"/24cm (approx 59 rows; take note for matching vest front). Place sts on holder. Break off yarn, leaving a long tail for sewing pocket to garment.

Left Front

Cast on 47 (55) sts.

Row 1 (RS) *K1, p1; rep from * to last st, k1.

Rep last row 11 times for seed st band.

Set-up row 1 (RS) [K1, p1] twice, k1 (k2tog), pm for seed st edge, p0 (5), work 30 sts in long cable and rib pat, p3 (5), pm for ribbed edge, [k1, p1] 4 times, sl 1 wyif—47 (54) sts.

Set-up row 2 K2, [p1, k1] 3 times, p1, k3 (5), work 30 sts in long cable and rib pat, k0 (5), [k1, p1] twice, k1.

Cont in pat as est, working 48 (60) rows of cable pat beg with row 1 (19).

Pocket ribbing

Row 1 (RS) [K1, p1] twice, k1, p0 (5), k4, pm for pocket ribbing, [k1, p1] 5 times, k2tog, [k1, p1] 5 times, pm, k4, p3 (5), [k1, p1] 4 times, sl 1 wyif—46 (53) sts.

Row 2 K2, [p1, k1] 3 times, p1, k3 (5), p4, [p1, k1] 10 times, p5, k1 (6), [p1, k1] twice.

Work 7 rows more in pat as est.

Next row (WS) K2, [p1, k1] 3 times, p1, k3 (5), p4, bind off next 21 sts, p4, k1 (6), [p1, k1] twice.

Join pocket to vest

Next row (RS) Work in pat to 1 st before bound-off sts. Place pocket with RS facing behind vest front and work that st together with 1 st from pocket. Work sts from holder, cont with cable pat row 29 sts 5 through 26, work 1 st from vest together with last st from pocket, work in pat to end—47 (54) sts.

Cont to work in pat as est until front measures 15 (17)"/38 (43)cm from beg, ending with a WS row.

Side shaping

Dec row (RS) Work 5 sts in seed st, k2tog (p2tog), work in pat to end.

Rep dec row every 6th row twice more—44 (51) sts.

Work even in pat as est until front measures 18 (20)"/46 (51)cm from beg, ending with a WS row.

Shape Armhole

Next row (RS) Bind off 4 (5) sts (one k st on needle), [p1, k1] twice, pm for seed st armhole edge, work in pat to end—40 (46) sts.

Work even in pat as est until armhole measures 6½ (7½)"/16.5 (19)cm, ending with a RS row.

Hooded Vest

Neck Shaping

Next row (WS) Work 9 sts in rib and place on holder, bind off next 5 (7) sts, work in pat to end.

Dec row (RS) Work in pat to last 3 sts, k2tog, k1.

Rep dec row every RS row 4 times more—21 (25) sts.

Shoulder shaping

Short row set 1 (WS) Work 15 (19) sts in pat, w&t; work to end of row.

Short row set 2 Work 10 (13) sts in pat, w&t; work to end of row.

Short row set 3 Work 5 (7) sts in pat, w&t; work to end of row.

Next row Work in pat as est to end.

Place sts on holder.

Right Front

Cast on 47 (55) sts.

Row 1 (RS) *K1, p1; rep from * to last st, k1.

Rep last row 11 times for seed st band.

Set-up row 1 (RS) [K1, p1] 4 times, k1, pm for ribbed edge, p3 (5), work 30 sts in long cable and rib pat, p0 (5), pm for seed st edge, [k1, p1] twice, k1 (k2tog)—47 (54) sts.

Set-up row 2 [K1, p1] twice, k1, p0 (5), work 30 sts in long cable and rib pat, k3 (5), [k1, p1] 4 times, sl 1 wyif.

Cont in pat as est, working 48 (60) rows of cable pat beg with row 1 (19).

Pocket ribbing

Row 1 (RS) [K1, p1] 4 times, k1, p3 (5), k4, pm for pocket ribbing, [k1, p1] 5 times, k2tog, [p1, k1] 5 times, pm, k4, p0 (5), [k1, p1] twice, k1—46 (53) sts.

Row 2 [K1, p1] twice, k1 (6), p4, [p1, k1] 10 times, k1, p4, k3 (5), [k1, p1] 4 times, sl 1 wyif.

Work 7 rows in pat as est.

Next row (WS) [K1, p1] twice, k1 (6), p4, bind off next 21 sts, p4, k3 (5), [k1, p1] 4 times, sl 1 wyif.

Join pocket to vest

Next row (RS) Work in pat to 1 st before bound-off sts. Place pocket with RS facing behind vest front and work that st together with 1 st from pocket. Work sts from holder, cont with cable pat row 29 sts 5 through 26, work 1 st from vest together with last st from pocket, work in pat to end—47 (54) sts.

Cont to work in pat as est until front measures 15 (17)"/38 (43)cm from beg, ending with a WS row.

Side shaping

Dec row (RS) Work in pat to last 7 sts, ssk (p2tog tbl), work 5 sts in seed st.

Rep dec row every 6th row twice more—44 (51) sts.

Work even in pat as est until front measures 18 (20)"/46 (51)cm from beg, ending with a RS row.

Shape armhole

Next row (WS) Bind off 4 (5) sts (one k st on needle), [p1, k1] twice, pm for seed st armhole edge, work in pat to end—40 (46) sts.

Work even in pat as est until armhole measures 6½ (7½)"/16.5 (19)cm, ending with a WS row.

Neck shaping

Next row (RS) Work 9 sts in rib and place on holder, bind off next 5 (7) sts, work in pat to end.

Dec row (WS) Work in pat to last 3 sts, p2tog tbl, p1.

Rep dec row every WS row 4 times more—21 (25) sts.

Shoulder shaping

Short row set 1 (RS) Work 15 (19) sts in pat, w&t; work to end of row.

Short row set 2 Work 10 (13) sts in pat, w&t; work to end of row.

Short row set 3 Work 5 (7) sts in pat, w&t; work to end of row.

Next row Work in pat as est to end.

Place sts on holder.

Finishing

Block pieces to measurements. Join shoulder seams using 3-needle bind-off. Sew side seams, starting 6"/15cm from lower edge. Sew pocket linings on WS.

Hood

Row 1 With RS facing, using first ball of yarn, starting at right front, work 9 sts rib from holder, pick up and k18 (20) sts along front neck, 18 (19) sts to center of back neck. Using 2nd ball of yarn, pick up and k18 (19) sts along rem half of back neck, 18 (20) sts along front neck, and pick up and k9 sts rib from holder (remembering to sl 1 wyif on last st)—90 (96) sts.

Rows 2, 4 and 6 Work 9 sts in rib, p to center, TY, p to last 9 sts, work 9 sts in rib.

Row 3 Work 9 sts in rib, k to center, TY, k to last 9 sts, work 9 sts in rib.

Row 5 Work 9 sts in rib, k4, [ssk, k1] twice, ssk, k12, ssk, k10 (13), TY, k10 (13), k2tog, k12, k2tog, [k1, k2tog] twice, k4, work 9 sts in rib—82 (88) sts.

Row 7 Work 9 sts in rib, k32 (35), TY, k32 (35), work 9 sts in rib.

Row 8 Work 9 sts in rib, p32 (35), TY, p32 (35), work 9 sts in rib.

Rep rows 7 and 8 until hood measures 4"/10cm from neck edge, ending with a WS row.

Inc row (RS) Work 9 sts in rib, k32 (34), kfb, TY, kfb, k32 (34), work 9 sts in rib.

Rep inc row every 12 rows 3 times more—90 (96) sts.

Work even as est until hood measures 9¾"/25 cm from pick-up, ending with a WS row.

Dec row (RS) Work in pat to 2 sts before center, k2tog, ssk, work in pat to end.

Rep dec row every RS row 15 times more—58 (64) sts.

Place half the sts on each of 2 needles. With RS together, join using 3-needle bind-off.

Sew fastener to front as desired. ∎

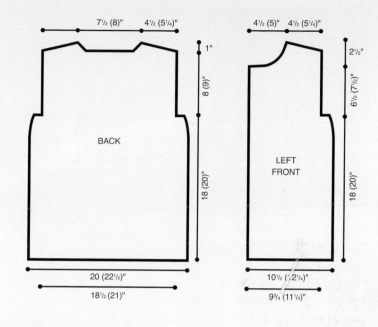

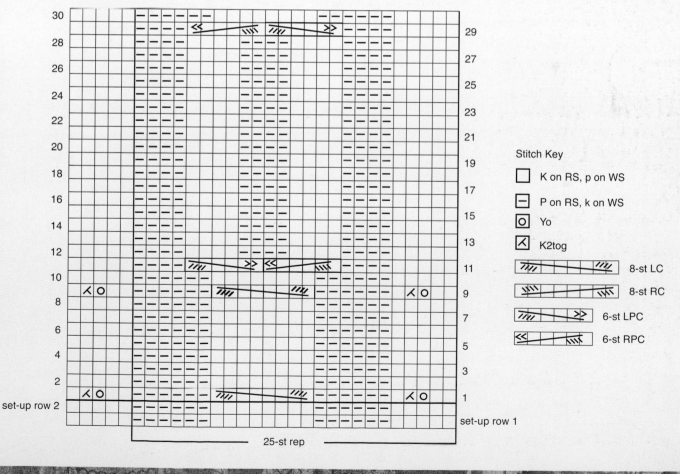

Stitch Key

☐ K on RS, p on WS

– P on RS, k on WS

Ⓞ Yo

⬩ K2tog

8-st LC

8-st RC

6-st LPC

6-st RPC

Belted Cardigan Vest *(Continued from page 13.)*

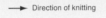

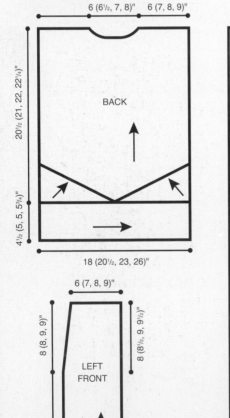

With larger needle and RS facing, pick up and k66 (70, 74, 78) sts evenly between markers. Work 32 rows of garter st pat (16 ridges). Bind off. Sew armband and side seams.

Front and neck band

With larger needle and RS facing, starting at lower right front, pick up and k103 (107, 111, 115) sts along right front to shoulder seam, 33 (37, 39, 43) sts across back neck and k103 (107, 111, 115) sts along left front—239 (251, 261, 273) sts. Work 3 rows of garter st pat, placing markers 88 (92, 92, 96) sts from each end.

Neck shaping

Row 1 K to 2nd marker from right-hand needle, k20, w&t.

Row 2 K to 2nd marker from right-hand needle, k20, w&t.

Row 3 K to 2nd marker from right-hand needle, k10, w&t.

Row 4 K to 2nd marker from right-hand needle, k10, w&t.

Row 5 K to 2nd marker from right-hand needle, w&t.

Row 6 K to 2nd marker from right-hand needle, w&t.

K to end, removing all markers.

Cont in garter st pat until 13 rows have been completed (at ends of band).

Inc row 1 K79 (81, 83, 86), *kfb, k7; rep from * 9 (10, 11, 12) times more, kfb, k to end—250 (263, 276, 287) sts.

Work 6 rows of garter st pat.

Inc row 2 K82 (85, 88, 92), *kfb, k6; rep from * 11 (12, 13, 14) times more, kfb, k to end—263 (277, 291, 303) sts.

Work 6 rows of garter st pat.

Inc row 3 K83 (87, 91, 96), *kfb, k5; rep from * 15 (16, 17, 18) times more, kfb, k to end—280 (295, 310, 323) sts.

Work 4 rows of garter st pat (16 ridges). Bind off.

Belt

With smaller needles, cast on 12 sts. Work in garter st pat for 58 (66, 74, 84)"/147.5 (167.5, 188, 213.5)cm. Bind off. ∎

Fair Isle Cardigan *(Continued from page 21.)*

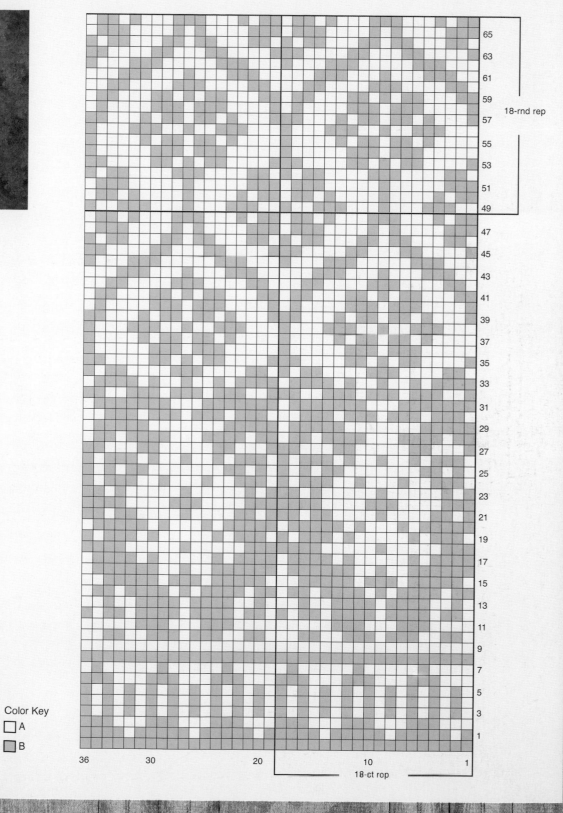

18-rnd rep

Color Key

☐ A
▨ B

Three-Button Cardigan (Continued from page 53.)

Dec row (RS) K1, ssk, work in pat to last 3 sts, k2tog, k1.

Work 2 (2, 4, 4, 6, 6) rows in pat as est.

Dec row (WS) P1, p2tog, work in pat to last 3 sts, p2tog tbl, p1.

Cont in pat as est, dec 1 st each side every 3rd row 3 (3, 3, 3, 2, 2) times more, ending with a WS row—49 (55, 55, 61, 63, 63) sts.

Work 4 (4, 4, 6, 6, 6) rows even in pat.

Inc row (RS) K1, m1, work in pat to last st, m1, k1.

Cont in pat, work inc row every 8th (8th, 8th, 6th, RS, RS) row 2 (1, 3, 4, 8, 13) times more—55 (59, 63, 71, 81, 91) sts.

Work even in pat until sleeve measures 8¼ (8½, 8½, 8¾, 8¾, 9)"/21 (21.5, 21.5, 22, 22, 23)cm from beg, ending with a WS row.

Sleeve cap

Bind off 3 (4, 5, 7, 11, 11) sts at beg of next 2 rows—49 (51, 53, 57, 59, 69) sts.

Dec row (RS) K1, ssk, work in pat to last 3 sts, k2tog, k1.

Rep dec row every RS row 12 times more—23 (25, 27, 31, 33, 43) sts.

Work even in pat until cap measures 3¾ (4¼, 4½, 4¾, 5¼, 5½)"/9.5 (11, 11.5, 12, 13.5, 14)cm.

Bind off 3 (3, 3, 3, 2, 4) sts at beg of next 2 rows, then 3 (2, 2, 2, 2, 4) sts at beg of foll 2 rows—11 (15, 17, 21, 25, 27) sts. Bind off rem sts.

Finishing

Block pieces to measurements. Sew shoulder seams. Set sleeves into armholes and sew sleeve and side seams.

Button band

With RS facing, pick up and k58 (64, 70, 70, 76, 82) sts evenly along left front edge. Work 14 rows of slip st ribbing, starting with row 2. Bind off.

Buttonhole band

With RS facing, pick up and k58 (64, 70, 70, 76, 82) sts evenly along right front edge. Work 6 rows of slip st ribbing, starting with row 2.

Buttonhole row (WS) Work 6 sts, bind off 3 sts, work 9 sts, bind off 3 sts, work to end of row.

Next row Work in pat, casting on 3 sts over each bound-off space. Work 6 rows even in pat. Bind off.

Neckband

With RS facing, pick up and k106 (106, 112, 112, 112, 112) sts evenly around neck opening, including front bands. Work 7 rows of slip st ribbing, starting with row 2.

Buttonhole row (RS) Work 3 sts, bind off 4 sts, work to end of row.

Next row Work in pat, casting on 4 sts over bound-off space. Work 5 rows even in pat. Bind off.

Using crochet hook, work 7 single crochet sts to finish off neckband and bottom front band edges. Weave in ends. Sew buttons opposite buttonholes. ∎

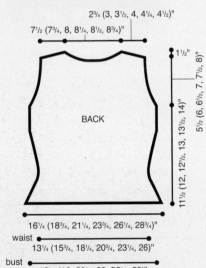

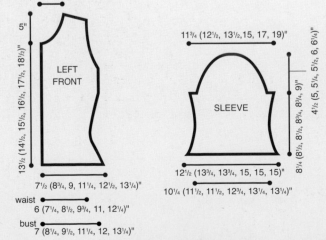

Cowl Neck Tunic (*Continued from page 61.*)

Bind off 4 (4, 4, 4, 5) sts at beg of next WS row, bind off 1 st at beg of next RS row.

Bind off 4 sts at beg of next WS row, bind off 1 st at beg of next RS row.

Bind off rem 4 (4,4,3,3) sts.

Left neck and shoulder

With WS facing, join yarn to shoulder and work 2 rows in pat.

Bind off 3 sts at beg of next WS row.

Bind off 2 sts at beg of foll 2 (3, 3, 3, 3) WS rows.

Bind off 1 (0, 0, 2, 2) sts at beg of next WS row.

Bind off 4 (4, 5, 5, 5) sts at beg of next RS row, bind off 1 st at beg of next WS.

Bind off 4 (4, 4, 4, 5) sts at beg of next RS row, bind off 1 st at beg of next WS row.

Bind off 4 sts at beg of next RS row, bind off 1 st at beg of next RS row.

Bind off rem 4 (4, 4, 3, 3) sts.

Finishing

Block all pieces. Sew shoulder seams. Sew side seams, leaving braided edge section open for vents.

Cowl neck

With RS facing and size 8 (5mm) 16"/40cm circular needle, starting at the right shoulder seam, pick up and k38 (40, 40, 42, 42) sts across the back neck and 40 (42, 42, 44, 44) sts across the front neck—78 (82, 82, 86, 86) sts. Pm and join to work in the round.

Rnd 1 Knit.

Rnd 2 *K2, m1; rep from * to end—117 (123, 123, 129, 129) sts.

Rnd 3 *K2, p1; rep from * to end.

Rep rnd 3 until cowl measures 5"/12.5cm.

Change to size 9 (5.5mm) needle.

Next rnd Purl.

Next rnd *P2, k1; rep from * to end. Repeat this rnd until cowl measures 10"/25cm.

Bind off very loosely.

Braided edging

Make 4 strips: 2 for lower edges and 2 for armholes.

Cast on 4 sts. Work in braid pat to fit. Bind off.

Block each strip and tack invisibly to lower and armhole edges.

Block garment lightly to measurements. ∎

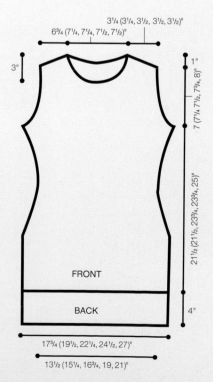

3¼ (3¼, 3½, 3½, 3½)"

6¾ (7¼, 7¼, 7½, 7½)"

3"

1"

7 (7¼, 7½, 7¾, 8)"

21½ (21½, 23¾, 23¾, 25)"

FRONT

BACK

4"

17¾ (19½, 22¼, 24½, 27)"

13½ (15¼, 16¾, 19, 21)"

Helpful Information

Abbreviations

approx	approximately	pm	place marker
beg	begin(ning)	psso	pass slip stitch(es) over
CC	contrasting color	p2tog	purl 2 stitches together
ch	chain	rem	remain(s)(ing)
cm	centimeter(s)	rep	repeat(s)(ing)(ed)
cn	cable needle	RH	right-hand
cont	continu(e)(ing)	rnd(s)	round(s)
dec	decreas(e)(ing)	RS	right side(s)
dpn(s)	double-pointed needle(s)	S2KP	slip 2 stitches together, knit 1, pass 2 slip stitches over knit 1
est	establish(ed)(ing	SK2P	slip 1, knit 2 together, pass slip stitch over the knit 2 together
foll	follow(s)(ing)	SKP	slip 1, knit 1, pass slip stitch over
g	gram(s)	sl	slip
inc	increas(e)(ing)	sl st	slip stitch
k	knit	sm	slip marker
kfb	knit into front and back of stitch	ssk	slip, slip, knit
k2tog	knit 2 stitches together	ssp	slip, slip, purl
LH	left-hand	sssk	slip, slip, slip, knit
lp(s)	loop(s)	st(s)	stitch(es)
m	meter(s)	St st	stockinette stitch
MB	make bobble	tbl	through back loop(s)
MC	main color	tog	together
mm	millimeter(s)	w&t	wrap and turn
m1	make one: with needle tip, lift strand between last stitch knit (purled) and the next stitch on the LH needle and knit (purl) into back of it	WS	wrong side(s)
		wyib	with yarn in back
		wyif	with yarn in front
m1P	make 1 purlwise	yd	yard(s)
oz	ounce(s)	yo	yarn over needle
p	purl	*	repeat directions following * as many times as indicated
pat(s)	pattern(s)	[ ]	repeat directions inside brackets as many times as indicated

Checking Your Gauge

Make a test swatch at least 4"/10cm square. If the number of stitches and rows does not correspond to the gauge given, you must change the needle size. An easy rule to follow is: To get fewer stitches to the inch/cm, use a larger needle; to get more stitches to the inch/cm, use a smaller needle. Continue to try different needle sizes until you get the same number of stitches in the gauge.

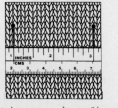
Stitches measured over 2"/5cm.

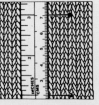
Rows measured over 2"/5cm.

Skill Levels

■□□□
Beginner
Ideal first project.

■■□□
Easy
Basic stitches, minimal shaping and simple finishing.

■■■□
Intermediate
For knitters with some experience. More intricate stitches, shaping and finishing.

■■■■
Experienced
For knitters able to work paterns with complicated shaping and finishing.

Knitting Needle Sizes

U.S.	Metric	U.S.	Metric
0	2mm	10	6mm
1	2.25mm	10½	6.5mm
2	2.75mm	11	8mm
3	3.25mm	13	9mm
4	3.5mm	15	10mm
5	3.75mm	17	12.75mm
6	4mm	19	15mm
7	4.5mm	35	19mm
8	5mm		
9	5.5mm		

Knitting Techniques

3-Needle Bind-Off

1. With the right side of the two pieces facing each other, and the needles parallel, insert a third needle knitwise into the first stitch of each needle. Wrap the yarn around the needle as if to knit.

2. Knit these two stitches together and slip them off the needles. *Knit the next two stitches together in the same way as shown.

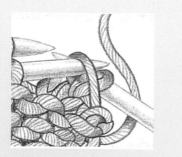

3. Slip the first stitch on the third needle over the second stitch and off the needle. Repeat from the * in step 2 across the row until all the stitches are bound off.

Yarn Overs

1. **Between two knit stitches:** Bring the yarn from the back of the work to the front between the two needles. Knit the next stitch, bringing the yarn to the back over the right-hand needle, as shown.

2. **Between two purl stitches:** Leave the yarn at the front of the work. Bring the yarn to the back over the right-hand needle and to the front again, as shown. Purl the next stitch.

Steeks

1. To work a steek, place eight stitches on a holder, then cast on eight stitches. When the body is complete, use the holder stitches plus picked-up stitches to work the band or the sleeve.

2. Pick up stitches through the inside loop of the first stitch before the steek by inserting the needle into the stitch and wrapping the yarn around the needle.

3. Once the steek is trimmed to a two-inch width, fold it back and sew in place with a finer yarn. Overcast the steek in one direction and then in the other direction as shown.

Knitting Techniques (continued)

Kitchener Stitch (Grafting)

1. Insert tapestry needle purlwise (as shown) through first stitch on front needle. Pull yarn through, leaving that stitch on knitting needle.

2. Insert tapestry needle knitwise (as shown) through first stitch on back needle. Pull yarn through, leaving stitch on knitting needle.

3. Insert tapestry needle knitwise through first stitch on front needle, slip stitch off needle and insert tapestry needle purlwise (as shown) through next stitch on front needle. Pull yarn through, leaving this stitch on needle.

4. Insert tapestry needle purlwise through first stitch on back needle. Slip stitch off needle and insert tapestry needle knitwise (as shown) through next stitch on back needle. Pull yarn through, leaving this stitch on needle.

Repeat steps 3 and 4 until all stitches on both front and back needles have been grafted. Fasten off and weave in end.

I-Cord

Cast on about three to five sitches. *Knit one row. Without turning the work, slip the stitches back to the beginning of the row. Pull the yarn tightly from the end of the row. Repeat from the * as desired. Bind off.

Crochet Chain Cast-On

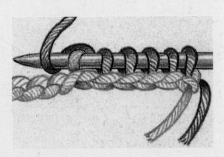

With waste yarn, make a crochet chain a few stitches longer than the number of stitches to be cast on. With main yarn, pick up one stitch in the back loop of each chain. To knit from the cast-on edge, carefully unpick the chain, placing the live stitches one by one on a needle.

Distributors

To locate retailers of Noro yarns, please contact one of the following distributors:

AUSTRALIA/NEW ZEALAND
Prestige Yarns Pty Ltd
P.O. Box 39
Bulli, New South Wales 2516
Tel: +61 24 285 6669
info@prestigeyarns.com
www.prestigeyarns.com

CANADA
Diamond Yarn Ltd
155 Martin Ross Avenue
Unit 3
Toronto, Ontario M3J 2L9
Tel: 001 416 736 6111
Fax: 001 416 736 6112
www.diamondyarn.com

DENMARK
Fancy Knit
Hovedvjen 71
8586 Oerum Djurs, Ramten
Tel: +45 59 4621 89
roenneburg@mail.dk

FINLAND
Eiran Tukku
Makelankatu 54B
00510 Helsinki
Tel: +358 503460575
maria.hellbom@eirantukku.fi

FRANCE
Plassard-Diffusion
La Filature
71800 Varennes-sous-Dun
Tel: +33 (0) 385282828
Fax: +33 (0) 385282829
info@laines-plassard.com

GERMANY / AUSTRIA / SWITZERLAND/ BELGIUM / NETHERLANDS/ LUXEMBOURG
Designer Yarns
Welserstrasse 10g
D-51149 Koln
Tel: +49 (0) 2203 1021910
Fax: +49 (0) 2203 1023551
info@designeryarns.de

JAPAN
Eisaku Noro & Co Ltd
55 Shimoda Ohibino Azaichou
Ichinomiya, Aichi 491 0105
Tel: +81 586 51 3113
Fax: +81 586 51 2625
noro@io.ocn.ne.jp
www.eisakunoro.com

NORWAY
Viking of Norway
Bygdaveien 63
4333 Oltedal
Tel: +47 51611660
Fax: +47 51616235
post@viking-garn.no
www.viking-garn.no

RUSSIA
Fashion Needlework
Evgenia Rodina, Ul. Nalichnaya, 27
St. Petersburg 199226.
Tel: +7 (812) 928-17-39,
(812) 350-56-76, (911) 988-60-03
knitting.info@gmail.com
www.fashion-rukodelie.ru

SPAIN
Oyambre Needlework SL
Balmes, 200 At. 4
08006 Barcelona
Tel: +34 (0) 93 487 26 72
Fax: +34 (0) 93 218 6694
info@oyambreonline.com

SWEDEN
Hamilton Yarns
Storgatan 14
64730 Mariefred
Tel/Fax: +46 (0) 1591 2006
www.hamiltondesign.biz

UK & EUROPE
Designer Yarn Ltd
Units 8–10
Newbridge Industrial Estate
Pitt Street
Keighley BD21 4PQ
Tel: +44 (0)1535 664222
Fax: +44 (0)1535 664333
alex@designeryarns.uk.com
www.designeryarns.uk.com

USA
Knitting Fever Inc
315 Bayview Avenue
Amityville, New York 11701
Tel: 001 516 546 3600
Fax: 001 516 546 6871
www.knittingfever.com

Index